Stone Time

Stone Time

Southern Utah:
A Portrait and a Meditation

T. H. WATKINS

With a Preface by Terry Tempest Williams

CLEAR LIGHT PUBLISHERS
SANTA FE, NEW MEXICO

Clear Light Publishers
823 Don Diego
Santa Fe, New Mexico 87501

Library of Congress Cataloging-in-Publication Data

Watkins, T. H. (Tom H.), 1936-
    Stone time, southern Utah : a portrait & a meditation / T.H. Watkins.
    p. cm.
    ISBN 0-940666-53-7 : $34.95
    1. Utah—Pictorial works. 2. Utah—Description and travel.
  I. Title.
F827.W38 1994
917.92-dc20   94-17389
                                          CIP

First Edition
10 9 8 7 6 5 4 3 2 1

Clear Light Publishers, in cooperation with the American Forestry Association, has planted trees to replace those used to manufacture these books.

All royalties from this book will support the conservation programs of The Wilderness Society.

Small portions of the text of this book first appeared in different forms in *Audubon* and *Wilderness* Magazines.

Preceding pages – Half-title: Wind circles in the Dirty Devil River canyons.
Title: Looking toward Square Top Butte, Reds Canyon, San Rafael Swell.

Printed in Canada

This one is for the Trapper

Preface

The "ultimate truth is so simple," writes Ramana Maharshi. "It is nothing more than being in the pristine state." T. H. Watkins understands this place of truth, the wisdom and necessity of wildness. He is our own sage who writes us back into the country we love – in this instance, the wildlands of southern Utah, where he confesses "I have found the very home of my heart." *Stone Time* becomes a memoir, a "baptism of discovery" lived and written by one of the great advocates of American wilderness who has chosen to immerse himself in the beauty and mystery of the Colorado Plateau. He is a literary pilgrim returning again and again to "touch the stone" and contemplate how a lizard "looks out upon the world of sun and hard edges." Watkins is a deeply disciplined man who respects the history of rocks and finds both his humanity and humility in the isolated canyons of Escalante or the wide expanse of Muley Point. He takes his vision outside so that we might remember inside through "the language of memory" how it is that we have strayed so far as a society from all that is essential: Earth. Fire. Water. Air.

Perhaps it is the gift of a good scribe to take on the character of the landscape he inhabits. Watkins's perspective is tough and tender at

By Terry Tempest Williams

once, like the desert, like Coyote. Expect the full range from this man. He knows how to listen and he knows when to speak. His words, his images, remind us that poetry and politics need not be separate. To describe the lands we love is to defend them.

I love Tom Watkins. He is one of our cherished elders who carries the history of the conservation movement in his bones. He will not let us forget the spiritual ties that bind us to the land and to each other. I have sat across the table from him during rigorous meetings of the Governing Council of The Wilderness Society where environmental policy was being debated and discussed. He never wavered. He is not afraid of raising his voice in the name of principles. He is not a man of compromise. And we have walked in silences and in gentle conversation in beautiful places: an autumn afternoon in the Adirondacks, in Yosemite, in Utah. The shape of his mind inspires me and I am grateful for his mentoring. We cannot overestimate the power of this kind of leadership, to touch stone.

Let us read T. H. Watkins with delight and follow his footprints into Utah wilderness remembering a "solitude replete with connections and the clamoring of life," the wild-heart country of redrocks and ravens.

Invocation

*S*tone time has a separate measure. There are no clocks to mark its passage, no lexicon of hours by which to define its parameters. We make a lot of guesses, though, as if our estimates somehow were required to invest these works of earth with meaning. Bravely, we try to measure the years out in the rocks. Call it Jurassic, we say, and wrap up a few dozen million years; this is Permian, we claim, and encompass a universe of time. If stones could laugh, they would. Maybe real time is too much of a terror to be embraced without the labels with which we try so hard to pin it down. And maybe we have been thinking about it all wrong to begin with. "Chaos is the law of nature," Henry Adams wrote. "Order is the dream of man." In the darkest portion of the night in this country, when the moon hides on the other side of the world and only the stars wink back at you with their ice-eyes, when the solid darkness of the unseen walls and the landscape all around you makes you feel as if you are floating in a void, you can, if you concentrate long enough, imagine that you are peering so deeply into the tunnel of space that you can discern that farthest distance where the universe starts to bend, one curve in the long ellipse that turns Creation back in on itself — and with it all that we think we know of time. So considered, time is chaos given order not by human measure but by the mute imperatives of the universe itself, and it possesses no beginning and no end, only process.

Any lizard knows this. Its eye looks out upon the world of sun and hard edges, sees there much of what we see; but the reptilian gaze turns inward, too, as ours does not, looks back down a corridor of time to that moment when some stones and all lizards were young, and humankind was as yet ungraced by the breath of Creation. Nevertheless, there never has been anything in a lizard's eye compelling enough, it seems, to stop us in the pursuit of blind convictions, and it does not stop us here in the land of stone time, either. We not only persuade ourselves that we can take the human measure of

Trail in the Escalante River Canyon.

I

inhuman time, we go further, and scribe the bounds of exploitation. This much is ours to use, we say, and that, and that. Listen: are the stones laughing yet?

That which we do not deign to use and use up we leave for what we call wilderness. There are those whose job it is to find it, mark it, make it visible in a boundaried age. They check the maps, walk around in the country, lay it all out in finely drawn schemata. Yet they often seem to want to get it wrong. How else explain the wildness that has vanished from their charts? Exactly where, on such pages, does wilderness begin and end? There are better ways to measure and to use, and none rely on what we think we know. Here is one: Find a hidden canyon twisting in the sun, walk into its coils and climb until it narrows to a slit. Rest against the rock. Put out a hand and push against the fabric of the stone until it hurts. Feel it then: feel the weight of stone time.

Difficult as it is to know, stone time is your time, too. Stone and sky and water speak the language of memory. You may not understand memory here, but you cannot escape it. You can escape the hours of your life counted out like pennies, find refuge from the temple of your measured days, but you cannot escape the oldest memories we have. They are all around you in the ancient library of the bare and scoured rock, the volumes stacked on edge, then twisted and carved and slashed and broken, incised by the rivers, cleansed and polished by the wind. Look long and closely enough and you will find fossil memories so distant from known human experience that only the double helix of life itself preserves them. There are closer memories to be found on the stone, too, the mute articulations of the people who have vanished, the Anasazi, the Ancient Ones. Cabalistic geometry, stick creatures, ancestral gods play upon your mind, while seductive neolithic whispers murmur in your blood, almost as loud as the clamoring of your heart as you test it against the meandering challenge of the canyon. You are alone, here in this narrow, secret place. You are not alone, here in this narrow, secret place.

Solitude, like poetry, like the West (as poet Archibald MacLeish reminded us), is a country in the mind. God knows, you can be unspeakably alone standing on a city street corner, the pedestrian river parting around your body like rushing water being split by a rock, the barking of automobiles, the growling of trucks a kind of natural force, like the sound of white water rapids or a high wind. But that is an internalized solitude, a fearful and niggardly thing, cutting all connections, hoarding your perceptions behind a shell of indifference. It is not even solitude; it is the most genuine loneliness.

There is no room for such indulgences in the land of stone time. Here, the solitude is replete with connections and the clamoring life all around you, the wide sky behind the piled-cotton clouds pulsing with the depthless indigo of the troposphere, the sculpted redrock walls stained with desert varnish like the big, careless splashes of a large-souled painter, the trembling rustle of cottonwood leaves, the incomparable perfume of big sage rubbed between the fingers, the chuckle of river-sounds, the keening cry of an eagle, the tumbling-down notes of a canyon wren's song — all this demands an acceptance of the possible. Everything here is expectation, the premonition that even the ordinary is likely to be invested with such shining individuality that it takes on the character of the remarkable, the rare, the awesome. Unless the potential for surprise has been leached from you, you cannot be lonely here, merely solitary in your humanness.

And sometimes you get a message. In your wanderings, perhaps you are lucky enough to encounter a mule deer browsing in the shade of an enormous old cottonwood — a big doe whose muted gray-brown hide makes her almost invisible in the mottled light beneath the tree. You slow your pace, as if you were moving under water, mesmerized by the sight of this sleek wild thing. You get very close before she raises her head and looks straight into your eyes for a long, tremulous moment before she bounds away, appearing and disappearing repeatedly with each impossibly graceful leap through the brush until she is lost to sight, a dream to be remembered.

Connections. Plato defined human beings as two-legged animals without feathers. Even in the swarm of the cities we reflect that animal nature — even if we refuse to acknowledge it and at the same time pervert it with the peculiarly human instinct for conscious cruelty. Savagery is, perhaps, a function of intelligence, but if so it is not something from which we should derive much gratification. In this wild country it is possible to encounter and truly experience the sweet reality of other kinds of intelligence, minds more precisely tuned to the knowledge that echoes through the corridors of evolution, telling us that none of us is alone on this cooling cinder. If we allow ourselves to put aside our arrogance long enough, perhaps we can read the lesson written in the eyes of lizards and deer deep in the land of stone time: this world and its creatures were not presented to us; we were joined to them in the exquisite saraband of life. The arrangement was never meant to be a conquest, and it is more deeply complex than a responsibility. It is a sharing.

So speaks the world of stone time. Come listen.

Part I: Discoveries

Sometimes I think I was born to deserts. I don't mean to suggest that my poor mother was forced to pop me out in a patch of creosote bush somewhere in the middle of the Mojave. I was born in a hospital in Loma Linda, California, just like normal people – even if the Seventh Day Adventist doctor who brought me forth laid me on my mother's stomach, then dropped to his knees and prayed over my yowling little body with the rest of the attendants for a while before cutting the cord and handing me over. So I was told by my still outraged mother in later life, at any rate; she thought it was an incredibly dangerous thing to have done, to have left me unattended so soon after birth while petitions were sent heavenward, though I wonder if perhaps it didn't do me some good in the long run.

That does not explain my affinity for deserts, but maybe this does: I have two important landscapes of memory from my childhood – that of the seashore and that of the desert. The shore was a long ribbon where the sand met the sea between Dana Point and San Clemente on the South Coast of California. Much of my childhood summers were spent on the beaches there in primitive communion with the elements of sun and wind and waves, and the experience almost certainly was an important force shaping my perceptions of the natural world and my place in it. In later years I tried to honor that legacy by writing a little book about those days, giving it the suitably euphonious title of *On the Shore of the Sundown Sea*, and by lending my voice to sporadic (and largely unsuccessful) attempts to keep that landscape of memory from being corrupted beyond recognition by the careless engineers of progress.

The other landscape lay over the long range of the San Bernardino Mountains, one of the transverse ranges that stretch across the middle of southern California east of Los Angeles. I was raised in the heart of what the boomers of the region still call the "Inland Empire," bounded on the east by the city

Moonrise over Comb Ridge.

of Ontario, on the west by that of Banning, with Riverside and Colton-San Bernardino filling up the southern and northern extremities respectively. Colton and San Bernardino, which nestled so closely together as to be nearly indistinguishable, were my towns, and behind them like the backdrop in an enormous theater were the San Bernardinos. On the other side of that back-drop was the desert, the Mojave (though the folks in Arizona, refusing to pay decent homage to the Spanish language that named the desert, insist on spelling it Mohave), an extraordinary sweep of country that made up much of San Bernardino County, the largest county in the United States. My moth-er and father loved desert country nearly as much as they did the shore, and during intermittent weeks and weekends of any given year, the family would pile into our big old Buick and cross the mountains through Cajon Pass, up through the dusty hamlet of Victorville, then with the air pressure in the tires lowered to improve traction, off on to one rutted, sandy road or another into a country of cinder cones and hidden springs, primordial lava flows and ravines deep enough to be dignified by the term "canyon," forests of improbable Joshua trees and mountains made entirely of boulders jum-bled up in impossible piles, oases of palms, and oceans of dunes.

It was during those expeditions that I truly learned to love wilderness. The sundown sea of my childhood gave me abundant joy, a sense of free-dom and possibility, but it was an easy place, generous and forgiving; even the sea itself, its waves eternally flowing toward security, promised salva-tion. But this contrary landscape, this desert place of rock and sky, sere and implacable and forever challenging, gave up nothing easily. What there was to know of joy had to be earned by effort and concentration, sweat and a stubborn attention to every living moment, every detail. The degree of effort required to discover it enlarged the dimensions of joy – once found. The place both toughened my mind and at the same time opened it to a world whose beauty cheerfully defied conventional protocols. How could you call a Joshua tree beautiful? How could you *not?*

It gave me something else, this landscape. It gave me solitude. I was the oldest of six children raised in houses never quite big enough to hold all of us comfortably. As I was the oldest, more responsibility for the younger kids was thrust upon me than probably was entirely healthy (it nourished in me a lifelong addiction to control, among other things, which did not tend to endear me to those around me). Consequently, much of my child-hood was spent in an effort to escape both duty and the crowd, but it was difficult. I built a platform high in the branches of the big old elm tree in our backyard once, and that gave me sanctuary for a while. But then the tree had to be destroyed and with it my little refuge. Even at the shore, there were always people around, my parents, my brothers and sisters, friends and relatives, and total strangers circling at the edges of my space, forever clamoring for my attention, my concern, my duty. Not so in the desert. Here I could vanish – or, perhaps more accurately, I could make others vanish. Over a hill or into a gully, around the bend in a dry wash, behind an enormous boulder, and I could be suddenly, gloriously alone, the people in my life out of sight, out of sound, and if never quite out of mind at least not filling it then with the clamor of duty, guilt, love, hate, all the impediments in the complex mix of emotions and responses that attended life in a big family – at least my big family. In the desert I could experience the land and myself *in* the land with a freedom no other time and place afforded me.

It would be decades before I would have the wit to search out that joy again. From my high school days on, the world was very much with me, and as the years passed I gave myself entirely to duty and indulgence in the crowded worlds of cities and professions. I wrote about wilderness and wild country from time to time, ultimately went to work to save them, as I had tried to do for the sundown sea, but somewhere in my meandering journey I had lost the instinct to seek them out, experience them for myself and for what they could still give me. In the end, it was the desert of my youth that helped bring me back to at least a semblance of that earlier consciousness as I entered the mainstream of environmentalist concern.

In 1986, Senator Alan Cranston introduced the California Desert Protection Act, designed to establish millions of acres of designated wilderness in the Mojave and Colorado deserts, as well as upgrade Joshua Tree and Death Valley national monuments to national park status and establish one brand-new park – East Mojave National Park – on 1.5 million acres of mountain ranges, palm oases, Joshua tree flats, and canyon systems administered by the Bureau of Land Management (BLM). The Wilderness Society, for which I worked by then, was one of the architects of the legislation and an essential player in the great game of law that would bring it to reality. To support that effort, I revisited the desert with my father, wrote a book about it, *Time's Island*, and threw it into the hopper as my modest contribution to the cause ("We also serve who only sit and write," I once proclaimed archly). Largely because of the diligence, skill, and unearthly dedication of people like legislative stalwarts Norbert Riedy and Nancy Green of The Wilderness Society, after more than eight years punctuated by agitation and negotiation and compromise, periods of hope and eons of frustration, Congress finally appeared ready to pass the bill in the summer of 1994.

I would be ready to celebrate that moment with at least as much glee as anyone; after all, it would validate much of what my youth had been given over to. But my personal satisfaction would go beyond that limited application, however gratifying, for by then I not only had reacquired the trappings of an old affection, I had learned to put it in the context of a larger desert experience. I had, in short, discovered a new desert mistress, a landscape that seduced me in my seniority as deeply and profoundly as the California desert had captivated me in childhood. I would, I vowed, try to know this new place as intimately as I had known the California desert and do everything in my power to save it, too. I would, no surprise, write a book about it. This book.

I can thank my friend Trapper Henderson — a.k.a. John G. Mitchell — for this development, and hereby do. He is a writer, an environmental journalist who has been at this rather specialized trade longer than just about anybody in the business and does it better than just about anybody in the business. In the spring of 1988, I had hired him to do a long piece on the unprotected wildlands of the BLM in southern Utah for *Wilderness*, the magazine I edit for The Wilderness Society. I did not give Trapper the assignment out of any personal allegiance I felt for these lands; the fact was, I knew very little about them, except that their protection was an issue of some priority with The Wilderness Society and it was my function to see that such concerns were articulated in the magazine with style and substance, both of which Trapper possessed in abundance. He knew these lands fairly well himself, though, enough to insist that it was time I was introduced to them. He liked to quote the novelist and naturalist Edward Abbey at me on the subject. These lands, Cactus Ed had written, comprised "the least inhabited, least inhibited, least civilized, least governed, least priest-ridden, most arid, most hostile, most lonesome, most grim bleak barren desolate and savage quarter in the state of Utah — the best part by far. So far." Come along with him for at least part of his journey there, Trapper said. I might be surprised. So I did, more because I wanted to spend some time with my friend than because of any fervent desire to tramp around in wild country.

You have to understand something about Trapper and me (his nickname, by the way, is taken from what he claims is an ancestor, an old mountain man with whom Mitchell identifies entirely too closely). By 1988 we had known each other for nearly twenty years and been friends as long, bond-

Above and right: Escalante Arch,
Escalante River canyons.

ed by a shared love of books, magazines, writing, and beards, but it had been an urban acquaintance. We met when I was a struggling free-lance writer in San Francisco and he was the visiting editor from the East. As a former reporter for the now defunct *New York American* and science writer and editor for *Newsweek*, and then David Brower's successor as editor-in-chief of Sierra Club Books in New York, he was as glamorous as all get out, coming into San Francisco to report to his superiors at the Sierra Club two or three times a year, scattering writing assignments like a fool at a fire, consorting with high good spirits at the Eagle Cafe on the Embarcadero with the rest of us ink-stained wretches. Then he left the Sierra Club, and I moved to New York, where we continued our friendship in those deep city canyons, six years during which the closest thing to wilderness we ever got was sitting out on his deck overlooking Lonetown Marsh in southern Connecticut once in a while. Finally, I moved down to the District of Columbia, and from that point forward we consorted only in concrete. We, who had spent much of our adult lives writing about wild country – and, as editors as well as writers, giving each other *assignments* to write about wild country – had never been in wild country together. Now we would be, and I was looking forward to that a good deal more than just seeing the country itself.

By journey's end, I had learned that our friendship was sturdy enough to survive even the sound of my snores thundering up from the folds of a sleeping bag or Trapper's craven refusal to risk life and limb indiscriminately (he took to calling me "Brushpopper" because of my own predilection to go crashing off alone in a pale and largely futile imitation of my childhood into whatever wild tangle presented itself). I also learned that, friendship aside, he had been right to urge me into this country, because I came out of it nothing short of beatified. Although our journey lasted only a week, with not much time spent in any one place, it made an acolyte of me. With cameras, water bag, and backpacks, we aging and slightly decrepit adventurers spent a day and a half staggering around in Thompson Canyon in the Book Cliffs just north of Interstate 70, then two days in the Escalante canyons between the little towns of Boulder and Escalante off Utah Highway 12. We four-wheeled into the heart of Capitol Reef National Park, and from our camping spot there gasped our way up to the Strike Valley Overlook to gaze down upon Oyster Shell Reef and Tarantula Mesa and across to the Henry Mountains. We made quick side trips into Crack Canyon slicing through the San Rafael Reef, Negro Bill Canyon cutting up from the

Colorado River. Through the courtesy of the folks at Project Lighthawk, the "wings of conservation," we got a couple of hours of overflight that gave us a bird's-eye gander at the Kaiparowits Plateau, the Escalante, Paria, and Colorado rivers, the slopes of the Henrys. In our Jeep we rumbled out to Burr Point above the Dirty Devil River, gazed in open-mouthed astonishment at the multihued chasm that opened before us, a miniaturized Grand Canyon, then scrambled down to a bench a hundred feet below the rim of the canyon to spend the night. I was as happy in those few hours as I had been in years. Trapper remembered it, too. "Tonight, at Burr Point," he later wrote, "it is a blustery Devil under a west wind off the snow-capped Henrys, and all those miles of hot, red dust between here and the mountains cannot soften the chill. We have made our camp out of the wind on a ledge below the rim, salvaged our rations of tortillas and kabobs . . . and saluted the stars. Now the Brushpopper is making noises about descending fifteen hundred feet to the river, just to get warm.

"You don't have a flashlight," I tell him.

"He'll use the stars," he says. I know he's bluffing. He's all zipped up in his mummy bag, preparing to snore. Not quite. Now he wants to know if I know what.

"What, old Brushpopper?"

"The sky," he says. "The sky has no lid on it."

Well, I should be forgiven the self-conscious effort at folk poetry, I think. The country that Mitchell had shown me seemed to require some kind of acknowledgment, an indication that I had actually comprehended the dimensions of the raw beauty I had been privileged to witness. The rituals must be observed, homage paid. And, I knew by then, pilgrimages made. The wildlands of southern Utah were not going to be like so many — too many — other landscapes in my recent life, places that I had taken a look at then moved away from, satisfied that the memory alone would suffice. I wanted to know these lands, pry into their hidden places, walk where I could persuade myself no one else had ever walked before, at least not within the age of recorded time, take the measure of myself as well as the land. Be, perhaps, a child again, open to wonder and excitement, ready and willing to be blessed by the unbidden gifts of life.

I had no sooner returned from my trip with Mitchell than I was calculating how to get back. It took me more than a year, but in the fall of 1989 I found myself in a lumbering old Cessna 182, which moved through the turbulence over the Kaiparowits Plateau with all the grace of a drunk falling down stairs. At the controls was Brant Calkin, with his shimmering white crew cut and his weathered old-young face. Grinning delightedly, he watched my own face wince bravely with every sharp thump and downdraft. The plane was his pride, flying this country his joy, and he was having a wonderful time ferrying me up from Cedar City to Escalante while filling my left ear with the latest on what the Southern Utah Wilderness Alliance (SUWA, of which he was then executive director) was doing to frustrate all the minions of progress and exploitation in the Bureau of Land Management and the chambers of commerce and county governments of the country that opened up below us like an enormous relief map.

As we crossed over the Straight Cliffs, Calkin cut back on the throttle and the Cessna drifted down to the little finger of tarmac that served as the Escalante Municipal Airport. Once the plane was safely pinned to the ground with anchoring cables (the wind out here, Calkin explained, was sometimes strong enough to tear the cap off a beer bottle), he fired up one of the several cheap clunkers he kept on hand in airports scattered around southern Utah for use whenever he dropped into an area for purposes of agitation or exploration. We climbed into the gasping, smoking old Ford Falcon and rattled off on Highway 12 a few miles to a little bridge that spanned the Escalante River. This was where Calkin dropped me, promising to pick me up at the same spot three days later. I wrestled into my brand-new backpack, hoisted my camera bag and the five-gallon plastic jug of water I was hauling to avoid the dreaded giardia (I had not yet discovered the magical MSR state-of-the-art filter I now carry with me everywhere in the wild), and started upriver with that lovely, fluttery mix of fear and anticipation that still comes over me like a blush whenever I venture alone into wild country.

I had chosen the Escalante for this first excursion because it promised greater ease of exploration. In my mind I carried the goal of someday finding my way to the bottom of the Dirty Devil River canyons, but remembering that enormous, complex hole in the earth east of the Henry Mountains I knew that I was a long way from being ready for anything so ambitious. In the meantime, the Escalante would do for starters. Mitchell and I had camped here on a pretty little sandy bench by the side of the river on

Clouds over the San Rafael Desert.

*Storm over Strike Valley
and Oyster Shell Reef.*

our earlier trip, and I was determined to find the place again. I trudged along the river's edge, weaving around cottonwood trees whose leaves flashed yellow in the October light, past box elders and willows, over marshy patches of grass, and through tangles of sage and shadscale and reeds, encountering more often than I cared to small clots of cattle brought down to this more habitable place from the overgrazed grasslands of Boulder Mountain before the onslaught of winter. I waved my hat, hollered, threw rocks to get the critters out of my way. Slowly, stupidly, then with sudden crashing panic, the clots would move, galumphing down the bank of the river and across to the other side, destroying God only knows how much riparian habitat in their clumsy passage. Dank, steaming mementos in the form of cow pies the size of manhole covers were all around me.

I found my kindly nature severely tested, as it has been many times since in similar circumstances. These were living creatures and as such deserving of my human respect, and families and local economies all over the West, we are told constantly, depend absolutely on the cattle industry to survive in this harsh, arid country; and it is all part of our national heritage, I suppose, a legacy from the pioneer days, the last stand of rugged individualism and the irresistible myth of the cowboy, Sir Galahad with gumption. So the litany of rationalization goes. Still, such close encounters of the bovine kind make me understand why Edward Abbey fantasized about a day when all cattle found on public lands would be shot on sight. This, I freely admit, is a sentiment unworthy of a responsible environmentalist, which I damn well am, and I do not express such thoughts among my colleagues while taking part in policy meetings on important conservation matters – or, since my mama didn't raise no stupid children, while sitting around in western bars and coffee shops. But, given the fact that these stumbling, grass-greedy, river-wrecking, overbred hamburgers on the hoof contribute something less than 2 percent of the beef eaten by America's two-legged carnivores, I sometimes wonder if the range management policies of the government – especially the Bureau of Land Management – are not artificially preserving an industry whose days are dwindling down to a precious few, soon to be as miniken and dim as those of the carriage-making industry or the wonderful folks who once brought us Fels Naptha. And what sort of price is the land paying in the meantime? Such are the intemperate thoughts that come to a man

Looking down on the Escalante River.

17

competing for space with cows in wild country. After the last of the semi-wild bunch had been shooed out of my way, I finally made it to the river bench that I had been looking for. When Mitchell and I first found it, the sand had been smooth and clean as a billiard table, bordered on one side by the river and on the other by a stand of cottonwoods that provided welcome shade – just about as inviting a place as you could find. Now it was a mess – though not because of the cattle. At least one flash flood and maybe several had been through here since that first visit. A few unfamiliar rocks and driftwood polished like pieces of marble littered the sand, and every tree and bush in the area was wearing a nestlike collar of debris; some of the stuff was piled up to a height of four or five feet, testimony to the force and depth of water that had careened through the place. I looked up at the late afternoon sky that was slowly gathering clouds, and in a moment of unaccustomed prudence decided I would not put my bedroll on the bench down by the riverside, as we had before; there was too strong a possibility that I would wake up in the middle of the night clinging to the pilings of the little bridge downriver and praying urgently for flood relief. I moved a little inland instead, setting up my primitive camp at the edge of the cottonwoods, rigging a fly with my tarp, and rolling out my sleeping bag beneath it.

As the sun began its slide down to the horizon through a thickening curdle of sky, I heated up water for instant coffee, then a can of Dinty Moore beef stew (its beef from a feedlot somewhere in Kansas, I assured myself). I spooned up the stew directly from the can, accompanied it with chunks from a loaf of French bread, washed it all down with the coffee, getting from all this a peculiar and thoroughly unwarranted primitive satisfaction, as if I had somehow hunted down and killed my meal with a spear and a big rock, instead of picking it up at a superette in Escalante on the way in. When the sun was down and darkness came, I followed some other paleolithic impulse and gathered twigs and driftwood for a fire down on the bench near the river. I sat by the fire, took my hiking shoes and socks off, dug my naked toes into the clean, cold sand, watching light from the flames dance off the wall of the sandstone cutbank on the opposite side of the river. There was no sound but the crackle of the fire and the muted grumbling of the river. Not a bird sang. Not a tree branch rustled. I looked up and felt the looming darkness of the canyon's walls, though I could not see them. I could not see the stars, either. Even those that would have been visible in the rare patches of clear sky would have been lost now against the transient human glow of the fire, but I knew that if the skies cleared later that night I would see them, diamonds broadcast across the velvet of the moonless night in such profusion that it would seem that the billions of grains of sand on which I sat had exploded out from there clear to the edge of time. And so they did appear, after the fire had burned down to a tiny glow and just before a full moon rose like the bright eye of God and spilled a silver wash of light over the abstract curves and angles of the suddenly ghostly landscape.

As it happened, the threatened rain was no more than a patter on my tarp from the swift passage of a continent-sized cloud that blocked the moonlight for a time. The drumming sound woke me, then talked me back to sleep again. I rose a little ahead of the sun, cooked up coffee and instant soup while the sky was metamorphosed from gray to blue. As it crept toward the horizon, the moon slowly faded, like an unfixed photograph. There were not enough clouds left to paint a sunrise, and as the morning light increased, the shadows in this hollow by the river were as sharp as a draftsman's lines. When the sun had risen high enough to peek over the canyon rim, its hard, flat light seemed to be absorbed and then retransmitted by the redrock walls, which glowed now as if illuminated from within.

I stuffed my daypack with a two-quart bottle of water and a bag of home-made gorp, put on my beat-up old Australian bush hat, and set off upriver. Over the next two days, using the river bench as a base camp, I covered more wild country on my own than I had at any time since the California excursions of my youth. I encountered not another human being during all this time (though I did run into a few more cows), and every now and then I felt such a surge of unadulterated freedom with the realization of my solitude that it left me nearly breathless. This was pure and plain escape from everything that constrained my daily life, and I wanted to howl with the pleasure of it.

I hummed to myself instead, storing up the memories: A moment in the sky, when a pair of red-tailed hawks met, made passes at each other, wheeled about like acrobats for a few moments, then disappeared over the rim of Wingate sandstone two hundred feet above me. A territorial squabble? Something with sexual implications? I did not know enough of hawk behavior to decide.

Midmorning during the trek of my first day out, when the sun was so hot I was forced to strip to a T-shirt. I had been trying to keep to the banks of the river, but after a while the brush grew so thick as to be impenetrable so I took to the water. The river was about thirty feet wide, running fast, cold enough to stop the heart. It fought me, the current piling up against my thighs as I slogged upstream. I rounded a bend, and just ahead of me was a large beaver dam. The sight of it stopped me cold. I had not thought of beaver in connection with this country, even though I knew perfectly well that they were here, had always been here. But there was something so *manufactured* about this cunning pile of engineered brush and limbs and twigs with the Escalante's healthy flow pouring over it that it seemed out of place somehow, however natural it truly was. Something else considered *me* out of place, I soon learned. While I stood in the middle of the river taking in this unexpected, if entirely logical sight, the air was split by a raucous croak and a great blue heron that had been standing still as a stick not ten feet from me burst into flight and raced past me downriver, complaining loudly all the way. I had not seen the critter, and the explosion of its sudden presence scared the bejabbers out of me.

A natural amphitheater formed in the redrock wall maybe three-fourths of a mile up a side canyon through which a lively little creek ran down to the Escalante. After nearly an hour of clambering up through the brush of the narrow, twisting, vegetation-crowded little canyon, I reached this cool and wondrous place, shaped like an enormous band shell, maybe forty feet deep and sixty feet high and wide, its floor of hardpacked sand as smooth as finished concrete. I could hear the hiss of my own labored breathing here, and I kept as quiet as stone, fearing that any sound louder than the beating of my heart would somehow damage the delicate curve of rock that framed the hemisphere of sky outside.

The ecologically unlikely ponderosa pine rose maybe a hundred feet high at the apex of another narrow canyon grotto that I had decided to explore. Undoubtedly sprouted from one of the thousands of cones that got washed down from Boulder Mountain during heavy rainstorms, the tree thrust up like an enormous old sentinel amid a shadowy tangle of willows and box elders and other vegetation crammed into the tiny space. It was as removed from its own kind here as I was, solitary. I wondered if it, too, found a measure of joy in its solitude, but also considered it entirely possible that I was beginning to anthropomorphize a little too much.

Escalante Natural Bridge and Escalante Arch, two geological oddities (though not so odd in this country). The bridge, as sturdy and symmetrical as if designed by a consulting firm, provided a fat link from one side to the other of a V-shaped cul-de-sac just off the river. To get a good look at the thing, I had to cross the river at one of its deepest, fastest-flowing points,

Above: Beaver dam on the Escalante River.

Right: Slickrock wall, Escalante River canyons.

pull myself up the opposite bank by exposed roots, and pick my way through an eroded tangle of brush and boulders and mud-packed gullies to a large, shadowy, bowl-like declivity scooped out of the rock. At its far end, accessible by a treacherous but negotiable slope of slickrock, was a small, sandy place, a declivity in the bigger declivity. It occurred to me, as I struggled up to the sandy spot to sit for a while, that this also would be a nice, cool place for a mountain lion to come to rest in the heat of the day, and I kept my eyes peeled accordingly. I had never seen a mountain lion in the wild and half hoped that one was lurking around here, even while knowing perfectly well that it was probably not the best place for mountain lion-watching if I ever wanted to live long enough to play Nintendo games with my grandchildren. I found no cat, however, only the irritating remains of someone's campfire. I stayed long enough to catch my breath, eat some gorp, and drink some water, the bridge looming sixty or seventy feet above me. Escalante Arch was more accessible. A few minutes upriver from the bridge, I spotted it off to my left, carved out of the topmost edge of a spectacular sweep of redrock wall that swept straight up perhaps a hundred and fifty feet above the river, the blue sky winking through the narrow slot in the rock like a vagrant, insouciant eye.

The second night in camp. Since the day had been cloudless, after eating I pulled my bag out from beneath the tarp and placed it near the bank of the river. I crawled in and counted stars for a long time before falling asleep. Sometime in the core of the night a light woke me. For one crazed moment I thought someone was standing above me with a flashlight. But it was the moon, edging over rimrock and shining directly into my face. It grew brighter and brighter as it came into full view, until the sky itself seemed illuminated. Then the coyotes started their yipping, first one, then another, and another, until a chorus was being sent up into the night. I joined them for a while – they did not seem to mind – until the unmistakable cries of a mountain lion, its voice crooning the range from the whimpering of a sobbing child to the screams of a tormented woman, stunned us into silence. When the mountain lion finally stopped, the coyotes and I decided not to follow its act.

A final memory: of a beautiful, spacious opening between monolithic sandstone walls discovered during my downriver wanderings, a spot too wide and too lovely to be dismissed as just another hollow. Eager to see the wholeness of what I had found here, I climbed up one side of the valley through patches of prickly pear cactus and pygmy forests of juniper and piñon pine, brushing past the furry green plumes of Mormon tea and groves of head-high mountain sage so aromatic that my senses swam with the smell of it. When the vertical reach of the canyon wall stopped my ascent, I turned and looked back down on the valley from which I had started. What spread below me was nothing less than a huge natural park, its floor pale yellow with fields of grass dotted here and there with tamarisks, willows, mountain mahogany, bigtooth maples, and spreading Gambel oak trees, the cottonwood-lined river curving gracefully through the whole scene, its beaver ponds burnished like mirrors by the sun, its rills and rapids glittering like crinkled foil. I stayed there for a long time, wondering why it had taken me so long to embrace such wonder, before starting back down to the valley, past the piñon pine and junipers, through the blue-green groves of sage, inhaling their scent as if I were trying to intoxicate myself forever with the essence of the place.

If my trip with Mitchell had been the baptism of discovery, those three days along the Escalante River were the confirmation that sealed my fate. Worn out, scratched, sunburned, and dirty, I packed up and hiked back to the pickup point at the Highway 12 bridge. Calkin had promised to be there no later than the early afternoon. I sat on a fallen tree and waited, the world I was returning to beginning to crowd in on my mind – the speech that I had to give up in Moab the next day, the magazine issue that had to be attended to when I got back to Washington, the book still unfinished, all the other impedimenta of a life busier than it should have been. No matter. I knew I would be back. To this place particularly, but to other spots as well in this newly discovered (by me, anyway) universe of rock and sand and hidden surprises. In the meantime, I would learn all I could about it and its history and put my own personal and professional resources to the cause of protecting it. I had no choice, for here in this land of stone time it seemed that I had found the very home of my heart.

Overleaf: Scene along the Escalante River.

Above: Formation near Coal
Mine Wash, San Rafael Swell.
Left: Monolith at the mouth of
Negro Bill Canyon. Right: Bottle-
neck Peak, San Rafael Swell.

Overleaf: Looking toward
Sams Mesa above the Dirty
Devil River canyons.

Part II: Rock, Water, Sky

In order to truly comprehend this landscape, you either have to rise above it or crawl into its innards. It does little good to stand upright on its edge and look off to the gently curving horizons in an attempt to grasp either its scope or its complexity. All the horizons can tell you about is the dimension of sky that lies over the land, and while this is a compelling part of the whole, it is not the whole itself. The region under discussion here, after all, is embraced within the bounds of the Colorado Plateau, some 57,000 square miles of a still-rising blister on the earth encompassing nearly everything in Utah south of the Uintah Mountains and east of the Wasatch Plateau and folding in substantial portions of Arizona — including, most spectacularly, the Grand Canyon — and lesser though still significant parts of Colorado and New Mexico, even a small chunk of southern Nevada.

In this great uplift a miracle of creation has been going on for hundreds of millions of years. Upon a foundation of ancestral rock that congealed some 3 billion years ago from the original matter out of which the earth was made, the plateau has been assembled from layers of sediment deposited by huge inland seas that have come and gone in successive waves of inundation and retreat through at least 300 million years of geological time, from the Pennsylvanian Period that ended 280 million years ago to the Cretaceous Period that began 136 million years ago. One variety after the other, the sediments drifted down through all the murky, ancient seas, settling, drying to muds under the relentless prehistoric sun, compressing to rock from the weight of each following deposition — gray limestone of the Honaker Trail Formation from the early Permian, maroon Wingate sandstone from the middle Triassic, buff-colored Navajo sandstone from the lower Jurassic; red Entrada sandstone, creamy Dakota sandstone, blue-gray Mancos shale, a dozen more during those millions of years before the final

Cottonwood and monolith in Reds Canyon, San Rafael Swell.

sea (or at least the most recent) shrank down to the bitter remnant we have named the Great Salt Lake. All along, the multicolored layer-cake land repeatedly was raised up, folded, fractured, wrinkled, squeezed, wrenched about, and twisted during periods when the earth shrugged and twitched mightily from the pressures of volcanism or the slow, grinding collision of continental plates — building mountain ranges, collapsing whole regions into the hot darkness where magma boils and curdles, thrusting them up again.

All of this frightful activity continues today, of course, even if the only ongoing part of it readily perceived by humans is what the raw force of water can accomplish. In terms of rainfall, the Colorado Plateau is a thoroughly arid region, but no element has been more important to the physical character of this land of stone than water, which, with a little help from windblown sand and extremes of temperature, has been working on the plateau assiduously for eons and will continue to do so until every last portion of it is carried to the sea, bit by microscopic bit. This may take a while, since the land continues to rise, slowly, inexorably, inch by inch, providing ever more land to be worn away. The chief laborer in this nearly eternal task is the river from which the plateau takes its name — the Colorado, which flows 1,700 miles from the Laramie Range in Wyoming to the Gulf of California in Mexico (or would, if all the river's dams were removed); with all its big and little tributaries, the Colorado is the dominant river system in the entire southwestern corner of the country, draining an area one-twelfth the size of the conterminous United States. Most of the river system, however, lies within the geographic bounds of the plateau, and it is here that erosion's most spectacular work has been done, silt-laden water cutting through all the earth-colored layers and swells and reefs of stone, sculpting hoodoos and goblins, spires and monoliths, arches and bridges, carving narrow slickrock canyons, parklike hollows, yawning chasms. The result is a wonderland of beautiful and bewildering diversity — not only of landforms, but of vegetation, wildlife, and natural systems as well.

And there is no more diverse, bewildering, or beautiful part of the plateau than the canyon country of southern Utah that resides at its heart.

Begin at the top right (northeastern) segment of an imaginary topographical map and work your way down it in a southwesterly direction and you will encounter most of what gives the lands of southern Utah their splendid singularity. Where you start is the Tavaputs Plateau, the northernmost of several individual uplifts of land that lie within the larger uplift of the Colorado Plateau. On its southern edge, the Tavaputs ends in a wildly irregular half-circle marked by the Roan Cliffs and, just below them, the Book Cliffs, stairstep escarpments that together rise a thousand feet. Into the ramparts of the Book and Roan cliffs have been cut numerous small, intricate canyons, among them Sego, Turtle, Floy, and Thompson (where Mitchell and I tramped in 1988), and through eighty miles of the Tavaputs itself the Green River has carved a winding gorge that cuts the plateau almost precisely in half and in such spots as Desolation Canyon is nearly as deep and spectacularly layered as the Grand Canyon.

South of the Book Cliffs the land spreads out in an ever-widening fan. To the southeast is the Colorado River coming in past Grand Junction, Colorado, racing to its meeting with the Dolores. On the east bank of the Colorado, just below the merging of those two rivers and just above the town of Moab, the redrock spires and monoliths of Fisher Towers rise like a misplaced portion of Arizona's famous Monument Valley 125 miles to the south. A little farther down the river, below the complex of land that slowly rises to the flanks of the snow-splashed La Sal Mountains, a creek flowing west from the myriad springs and seeps that feed it drops more than a thousand feet from the Porcupine Rim to the Colorado. The little gorge the creek has made through layers of Navajo and Wingate sandstone is called Negro Bill Canyon, a place whose bosky creekside habitat provides one of the most significant riparian areas anywhere in the Utah wildlands.

Across the Colorado from Negro Bill Canyon are the extraordinarily ornate formations embraced within Arches National Park — 70,000 acres of natural arches, bridges, domes, spires, fins, caves, clefts, and ravines, most of them sculpted from sandstone whose colors range from white to salmon, pink, and blood-red. A few miles southwest of Arches, past whose eastern boundary it has flowed swiftly if not yet too deeply, the Colorado presents the first of its most accomplished canyonland efforts, impressive gorges through which the white-watered river tumbles vigorously, winking and glittering two thousand feet below gape-mouthed observers looking at it from Dead Horse Point or Grand View Point. At Grand View Point we are in Green River country again, too, the Green immensely powerful in its own right now, slicing a narrow, tortuous passage through Labyrinth Canyon and Canyonlands National Park to its confluence with the Colorado just above Cataract Canyon. From here, the Colorado flows through its last free stretch before spilling out into the beginning of the man-made reservoir called Lake Powell, "a river no more," in the gloomy but accurate words of environmental writer Philip Fradkin.

Back up at the top of our map, now, west-by-south west of the Book Cliffs, its top third bisected by Interstate 70, is the San Rafael Swell, another uplift of distinction. The swell, a kidney-shaped rise thirty miles wide and seventy long, is so distinct, in fact, that it very nearly comprises its own ecoregion. For one thing, most of its eastern and a good part of its southern extremities are walled off from the broad stretch of the San Rafael Desert to its south-west by the San Rafael, North Caineville, and Caineville reefs, ancient sand-stone intrusions – or plunging anticlines, as the geologists have it – that are jammed at a steep angle through the crust of the earth like more than seven-ty miles of enormous, stone-colored teeth jutting from the lower jaw of some unimaginable beast. On its western and northern edges, the swell is separated from the Wasatch Plateau by a wide tableland called the Castle Valley that ends abruptly in a series of cliffs and canyon systems plunging into the heart of the region. For another thing, the swell offers a few places – especially the "Black Box" of the San Rafael River and "The Chutes" of Muddy Creek – in which layers of Coconino sandstone are exposed; at 250 million years, these are some of the oldest rocks found anywhere on the Colorado Plateau. Finally, the swell contains probably the greatest variety of landforms of any given region in southern Utah – extensive mesas, like Sids Mountain, Cedar Mesa, Caineville Mesa, or the Mussentuchit Badlands; huge standing forma-tions like Tomsich Butte in Hondoo Country or Factory Butte on the swell's southernmost edge; smaller, more intricately carved forms, like Family Butte just north of Reds Canyon or the mushroom-capped hoodoos in the narrow, slotted draws and washes of the San Rafael Reef just west of the San Rafael Desert; rolling gray oceans of Mancos shale, like those surrounding Factory Butte and Caineville Mesa, and wide benches of sagebrush and piñon pine and juniper forests, like those along the Big Ridge and in Sinbad Country, so named because someone here was reminded of the place described in *The Arabian Nights* as a "valley exceeding great and wide and deep, and bound-ed by vast mountains that spired high in the air"; and canyons, like those carved by the upper San Rafael River and Muddy Creek, that many people feel are as complex and entrancing as anything you can find in the plateau (or *The Arabian Nights*, for that matter).

Family Butte, San Rafael Swell.

One possible exception to that claim is what the Dirty Devil River has produced just twenty miles to the southeast. The Dirty Devil has its source in the San Rafael Swell (Muddy Creek is one of its principal tributaries and contributes much if not most of the silt that gives the river its name) but almost immediately leaves it, flowing south through the sandy, sparsely vegetated San Rafael Desert, then the red-soiled flats of the Burr Desert crowded with dark green sage, and finally the redrock country of Glen Canyon National Recreation Area before emptying its load into Lake Powell. Along the way, the river has excavated one of the widest, deepest, most extensive, and least-known canyon systems in all of the Southwest — forty miles long, ten miles wide, and in spots as much as 2,000 feet deep, exposing wide layers of Wingate, Kayenta, and Navajo sandstone. The system includes eight major canyons coming in from the east or west of the shallow, southerly-flowing river, among the most colorfully named of them Poison Spring Canyon, No Mans Canyon, Robbers Roost Canyon (where, it is said, Butch Cassidy and his gang once hid out), and Happy Canyon. To stand at Burr Point above the middle section of the canyons, with the sun behind you and the wind clearing the air of dust, looking across to Sams Mesa, with a 150-foot butte poking up at its center, and beyond the mesa clear to the La Sal Mountains (or so you can persuade yourself), then two thousand feet down into the magnificent abyss, with the café-au-lait river snaking slowly through a maze of its own making, is to experience a definitive sense of the power of rivers and the character of earthly space.

Turn around and move a few miles to the west and your gaze will tend to travel up, not down, for above the sagebrush flats there looms a series of failed volcanoes, collectively called the Henry Mountains and featuring three major peaks running north to south — Mount Ellen at 11,508 feet, Mount Pennel at 11,320 feet, and Mount Hillers at 10,650 feet — with two small outcrops, Ragged Mountain and Bull Mountain, on the range's eastern side. All are versions of what are called lacoliths, which the authors of the report by the Utah Wilderness Coalition entitled *Wilderness at the Edge* describe as "huge blisters in the earth's surface, formed when molten lava, boiling upward from the under world, encountered a roof of sedimentary rock so thick and so tough that it could bend upward, forming a dome, without rupturing and allowing the lava to escape to the surface. . . . After the mountains were in place, erosion gradually removed the surface rocks, revealing the volcanic core of the range." And some range it is, an alpine wilderness set down in the middle of a canyonland landscape, a place

Fisher Towers from the Fisher Valley.

Hoodoos in the San Rafael Reef.

where sage gives way to piñon pine and juniper, then aspen, ponderosa pine, fir, spruce, even bristlecone pine, forests more appropriate to the Rocky Mountains or the Sierra Nevada than the middle of the flat, river-incised country of the Colorado Plateau – which explains why Mount Holmes and Mount Ellsworth, another two examples of the volcanic breed fifteen miles to the south of Mount Hillers, were dubbed the "Little Rockies" by John Wesley Powell and the members of the Powell survey in 1869.

On the western side, the Henrys slide down to a stairstep of piñon pine and juniper benches and mesas, including Swap Mesa and Tarantula Mesa, both of which overlook the Strike Valley and the toothy white line of Oyster Shell Reef and, beyond and above that, much of the Waterpocket Fold, a clifflike wall of Wingate and Navajo sandstone layers that were uplifted, bent, and fractured maybe 70 million years ago then worn into rounded, domelike forms along much of the ridge's eighty-mile length from just under Thousand Lake Mountain in the north to just above Lake Powell in the south. In a nearly waterless country, the Waterpocket Fold's ability to capture runoff from the cliffs in natural pockets, or tanks, in the rocks gave it its name, while the resemblance of the rounded stone forms of its northernmost extension to various state and federal government capitols inspired the naming of Capitol Reef National Park, which includes most of the long formation.

In the nearly thirty miles that lie between the 1,000-foot-high Waterpocket Fold and the Circle Cliffs on the east and the 2,000-foot-high Straight Cliffs on the southwest is a jumble of canyon country created by the Escalante River and the seeps, rills, and creeks that feed it, only a few of them big enough to be dignified by the term "tributaries." The Escalante itself has its headwaters in the Escalante Mountains to the west-by-north west, but several of its main creeks – Calf, Boulder, Sand, and Deer creeks chief among them – come down from the slopes of the Aquarius Plateau to the immediate north, an 11,000-foot uplift dominated by the broad reach of Boulder Mountain, whose eastward-facing slopes provide heart-stopping views back across the red, pink, and white monoliths of the Waterpocket Fold to the hazy blue wall of the Henry Mountains. The canyon system here is neither as broad nor as deep as that created by the Dirty Devil River, but there is no system anywhere in canyon country that is more accessible and more revealing of the varieties of life and beauty that these lands

View from the Wedge, San Rafael River canyons.

39

encompass. The main stem of the river, ranging in depth from ankle to waist, depending upon where the beaver have chosen to place their dams, winds sixty linear miles down from the mountains to Lake Powell through as diverse a mix of stone as anything you will find west of the Colorado line and north of a given point; all the layers of rock from the Moenkopi Formation at the cusp of the Permian Period to Dakota sandstone at the beginning of the Cretaceous are represented here in buttes and knobs and monoliths and slick red wall cliffs that plunge hundreds of feet from the topmost mesas straight down to the river, their faces blotched dark with desert varnish and glimmering with occasional seeps from the tops and bottoms of which sprout iridescent patches of green ferns and mosses. In the many side canyons, hidden waterfalls like Upper and Lower Calf Creek falls drop long ribbons of water into deep, glacier-cold pools surrounded by ferns and tamarisks and willows. Caves, alcoves, and slot canyons provide the shadow of mystery, and generously proportioned draws open up into parks where the sun bathes everything in a glowing wash of warmth.

The Straight Cliffs that mark the southwestern boundary of Escalante country also mark the northeastern boundary of the Kaiparowits Plateau, a huge scalene triangle with Lake Powell forming a baseline to the south and the Cockscomb, a 1,500-foot-high wall of uplifted sand stone cliffs, slicing down to meet it – a conjunction prevented only because the Paria Plateau comes in over the Arizona border to intervene. Within its 800,000 acres, the Kaiparowits features probably more pure wilderness – landscape "untrammeled by man" in the institutional poetry of the Wilderness Act of 1964 – than just about any other portion of southern Utah. For one thing, it is perhaps the single most arid place in the region, with no rivers and but a handful of creeks, few of those year-round; for the most part, only isolated springs provide enough water to support pockets of vegetation that relieve the harshness of this stony, desiccated maze of canyons.

Just to the northwest of this hot place of lichens and lizards begins one of the most impressive landforms in the West, the Grand Staircase, a series of cliffs, mesas, and plateaus that reaches all the way to the rim of the Grand Canyon and includes some of the most spectacular scenery anywhere in the world – much of it institutionalized in Bryce Canyon, Zion, and Grand Canyon national parks but most of it still unprotected in any form whatever. Here, relict grasslands survive on No Mans and Little No Mans mesas, two of the rare grassland regions in the West that have never known the relentless munching of sheep and cattle; here the Paria River and Sheep Creek

40

Desiccated tree, Arch Canyon.

slice canyons a thousand feet deep through the red sandstone of the Carmel Formation; here, the Blues, a badlands region made of Mancos shale, roll off to the edge of Table Cliff Plateau; here, Canaan Peak pokes 8,000 feet into the sky, the Paria Box spreads out in the bottomlands of the Paria River, and Box Canyon adds to the outlandishly sculptured fins and spires that ornament nearby Bryce Canyon National Park.

Our imaginary excursion ends now at the bottom portion of our imaginary map, a narrow fan of country running from Glen Canyon National Recreation Area to the Colorado state line between the Colorado River and the Navajo Indian Reservation. It may lack the spectacular quality of places like the Dirty Devil River canyons or the landform diversity of the San Rafael Swell, but this country has its own valid claims to distinction. Just across Lake Powell from the eminence of Mount Ellsworth, for example, is Mancos Mesa, 180 square miles of tabletop land surrounded on all sides by slick rock cliffs anywhere from 1,000 to 1,500 feet high. Part of it lies within Glen Canyon National Recreation Area, the rest of it in Bureau of Land Management territory, but all of it comprises the largest such mesa in southern Utah. Then there are the dozens of draws and gulches, washes and canyons that drain into the San Juan River along more than 100 miles of its length – Slickhorn Canyon and Grand Gulch south of Natural Bridges National Monument, for instance, or Mikes, Lake, and Castle canyons in the Nokai Dome, where spring-fed streams have exposed redrock walls that rival those of the Escalante. Nor does Comb Ridge compare poorly to any similar landform in the state; 600 feet high and running 90 miles north to south from the southern border of Manti-La Sal National Forest to just a hair above the San Juan River, this sandstone monocline – one layer of sediment rammed up over another, its eroded western edge forming the ridge – overlooks a broad wash that runs almost the full length of the monocline, filled with juniper, piñon pine, and sage and watered by Fish, Owl, and Road Canyon creeks, all of which help nurture one of the best riparian habitat regions south of Negro Bill Canyon. So do the seeps and springs of Arch Canyon, a vegetation-packed gorge that meanders northwest from the upper end of Comb Wash, growing narrower and deeper and more elaborately formed, with arches, bridges, eroded spires, and towering slickrock monoliths, as it cuts into higher and higher country before coming to an end in Texas Canyon just below Elk Ridge. Finally, there is Dark Canyon Plateau just south of Canyonlands National Park, at the southern edge of which the Monument Upwarp has raised so much underlying rock that erosion in

Dark Canyon, the principal canyon system in the region, has exposed some of the oldest layers of the Honaker Trail Formation to be revealed anywhere on the Colorado Plateau — as many as 300 million years of the earth's history lifted up and laid open like the pages of a gargantuan book.

It is all as Wallace Stegner described it in his famous "Wilderness Coda," then, "a lovely and terrible wilderness, such a wilderness as Christ and the prophets went out into; harshly and beautifully colored, broken and worn until its bones are exposed, its great sky without a smudge or taint from Technocracy, and in hidden corners and pockets under its cliffs the sudden poetry of springs." But within this sere and broken vastness there is more richness of life than one might think possible in a land with so little water and so much heat.

Vegetation, particularly in riparian areas, is remarkably diverse. Cottonwoods, tamarisks, piñon pines, and junipers are the trees most common throughout the Colorado Plateau, but manzanita, Gambel's oak, scrub oak, desert willows, single-leaf ash, and mountain mahogany are frequent, and in the upper elevations of many areas aspens and ponderosa pines are abundant. Mountain sage and desert sage, shadscale and ephedra, Mormon tea and milkvetch, rabbitbrush and black brush, serviceberry, snowberry, buffalo berry, and holly-grape are the most common shrubs, while cattails, reeds, and various sedges flourish along streamsides and various cacti, chief among them prickly pear and hedgehog, are scattered throughout the drier regions. Jimson weeds, asters, desert marigolds, desert paintbrush, sego lilies, goldenrod, lupines, desert dandelions, arrowleaf balsamroot, blanket-flowers, and other species provide a handsome celebration of wildflowers.

The critters that swim, creep, crawl, skitter, leap, and fly through the region are equally various. Fathead minnow, bluehead sucker, roundtail chub, red shiner, plains killfish, largemouth bass, green sunfish, and even brown and rainbow trout can be found negotiating the rivers and good-sized streams, joined by growing populations of beaver (river otters, once common, are long since extinct in the region). From under the rocks and across the sand speed whiptails, crevice spiny lizards, and sagebrush lizards, while western and diamondback rattlesnakes take shade under the same rocks. Significant populations of mule deer are seen almost everywhere, from the banks of the Dirty Devil River to the slopes of Arch Canyon. Much

Overleaf: Looking north to the Henry Mountains across Harris Wash.

Creek in Negro Bill Canyon.

smaller populations of pronghorn inhabit such areas as the sagebrush flats above Labyrinth Canyon and the western slopes of the Henry Mountains, and even smaller populations of elk can be found in the Tavaputs Plateau benchlands and the North Escalante River canyons and at other relatively high elevations. Desert big-horn sheep herds of varying sizes inhabit many parts of canyon country, particularly such portions of the San Rafael Swell as Sids Mountain, Mexican Mountain, and the San Rafael Reef. A reintroduced herd of bison are doing quite well, thank you, in the Henry Mountains. Mountain lions reveal themselves most often in the tracks they leave behind or the cries that they fling into the night, but they remain the largest wild predators left in most of the land (in some areas of higher elevation, though, such as Box Canyon adjacent to Bryce Canyon National Park, black bears can be found). Almost as shy as mountain lions, but a good deal more numerous, are coyotes, the big cat's closest competitors, whose spoor can be discovered in virtually every landscape and whose own music ornaments the night. Canyon wrens, swallows, magpies, Lewis's woodpeckers, western and mountain bluebirds, and any number of other small dinosaur descendants flit through riparian greenery or swoop along red canyon walls. Great blue herons, common mergansers, mallards, and blue-winged teal decorate rivers and ponds, while most of the raptor species find a good living throughout canyon country – including peregrine falcons, golden eagles, a few bald eagles here and there, great horned and burrowing owls, American kestrels, prairie falcons, and several species of hawks.

There is, of course, another critter that inhabits the land, one of the ape species, Homo sapiens by name (though some would maintain it has never moved much beyond Homo erectus). We humans are almost as ubiquitous as coyotes in the land of stone time, if a good deal less comfortable in our skins. Modern humanity is the only species that seems out of place here. Maybe that is because no humans of any vintage have been here as long as any wild species, or maybe it is only because we have made such a long, stubborn, and too often ignorant journey from the essence of what we once were to what we have since become.

Entrance to Happy Canyon, Dirty Devil River; Overleaf: Moonset over Factory Butte.

Part III: Artifacts

In a small canyon whose name I am not going to tell you in a region of southern Utah I am not going to reveal, I once came upon a huge wall of stone that curved over a little creek. On the narrow pile of talus beneath the wall and above the creek were a number of large sandstone boulders that had split off and fallen from the wall at some point in the geological past. Driven by some inarticulate curiosity, I waded across the creek and scrambled up the slope to the rocks. Scattered about the little site were tiny sherds of pottery, thin, clearly ancient. So, too, were the miniature ears of corn tucked into metates, or small depressions, that had been worn into two of the smaller boulders by the action of stone moving on stone to grind the corn into meal. And finally, at the rear of the largest boulder, impossible to see from the creek, was incised the antic figure of a horned and humpbacked creature sporting an erection nearly as long as the flute in his mouth. He seemed to be dancing as he leaned toward the coiled figure of a horned rattlesnake and played an eternal piping whose melody I could only imagine but which was no less powerful for that fact. Was the creature playing out of fear, to propitiate the snake and stave off disaster, or were he and the snake locked in some ancient ritual of shared creaturehood as lost to me and my kind as the song he was playing? I could not say, and it did not matter; to stand there and behold that painstakingly graven image was to share in a spiritual experience older than history, older than conscious memory, older than anything we yet know how to measure.

The image, I have since learned, was that of the god the Indians now call Kokopelli, the remnant figure of a prehistoric culture that once was dominant in this and much of the rest of the American Southwest. The artful Kokopelli, it was said, would travel from village to village with a sack of corn seed on his back (hence the humpback), teaching the people how to plant and nurture corn. When the crop was planted, he would dance through the fields playing his flute all night, and in the morning, the corn would have sprouted. But it

Pictograph and petroglyph panel, location undisclosed.

53

was not only corn seed that would get planted during the long desert night, it seems; that same morning, most of the young women in the village would find themselves mysteriously pregnant (hence the figure's erection).

The knowledge of what it was I had found has taken none of the magic from it. It remains as wonderful a mystery to me now as it was when I first discovered it. Nor was it the only such artifact I have encountered in the canyon country. On that same excursion, for example, not far from where I discovered Kokopelli, I also found a large panel of pictographs (paintings on rock) and petroglyphs (figures cut into the stone, like my Kokopelli) hidden at the base of a towering wall behind a high, narrow slab of rock that leaned out over the top of an enormous pile of talus. The panel could not be seen from any vantage point below, and I still do not know what inspired me to crawl up that slope to see what I could see. Once there, my effort was twice reward-ed, for maybe a hundred feet above me, almost invisible in a small declivity in the otherwise sheer face of the slickrock wall, were small stone granaries in which corn, piñon pine nuts, ricegrass, and other foods apparently had been kept. How the people who built them managed to do so in such a place was a question as impossible to answer as the meaning of Kokopelli's dance with the rattlesnake.

Such moments of serendipitous discovery have been granted to me repeat-edly, each one treasured. But I am hardly unique in the experience, which is why I no longer identify most of the sites I have found and photographed, even those that are probably well known by now. The simple fact is that too many of the wrong kinds of people know about such things already, and like most of those who care about this country I have taken a vow of silence, or at least of careful obfuscation.

The Bureau of Land Management and the National Park Service are similarly timid these days; in their newest maps, officials have announced, they plan to be a good deal less precise about where petroglyphs, paintings, artifacts, and rem-nant structures can be found on the federal lands within their jurisdictions — and with good reason. In 1987, the BLM calculated that at least thirty thousand archeological sites identified on public lands in the states of the Four Corners region — Utah, Colorado, New Mexico, and Arizona — had been damaged or looted. Much of this was mindless vandalism, the savage instinct to ruin some-thing for the sheer pleasure of it, but most of the worst mutilation was done by private and professional "collectors" who pillage ancient sites for profit, picking up pottery sherds and arrowheads, blasting out petroglyph panels with jackhammers and dynamite, using backhoes to dig out human bones from burial sites, tearing down granaries with crowbars to get at the ancient ears of corn hidden within. The fact that all this is very much against the law – specifically, the Archeological Resources Protection Act of 1979, which provides penalties of up to two years in jail and fines of up to $20,000 – does not seem to deter most of them. "We are a culture that lives by extracting uses and materials from the earth," John Daniels wrote in "Stealing Time," an article in the spring 1990 issue of *Wilderness*, "and it is inevitable that such a culture will produce pothunters. They are merely another kind of extractor, and their industry is of an all too familiar kind: they exploit the land for one of its non-renewable resources. Believing that whatever they have the gumption to take is rightfully theirs . . . they pursue their trade in the time-honored tradition of the American frontier. Their trade happens to be illegal, and the trade of gold miners happens to be legal, but in terms of the land there is little difference. The pothunters sell their valuables about as easily as the gold miners sell theirs, business goes on, and the land is diminished."

So are we. Such reckless pillage defiles the memory of a whole race of human beings whose shadow once lay hugely on this land. By tolerating such cultural mayhem, we reduce by just that much our own fragile humanity.

The history of the first people of the Southwest ended in stone and symbol. The stones are mute, and the symbols – all those spirals, squares, circles, dots, wavy lines, outlined hands, humanoid figures, stylized renderings of snakes, elk, deer, and bighorn sheep that ornament tens of thousands of individual stones and rock wall panels – inspire yet confuse us. In spite of more than twenty years of new scholarship, in the preface to the 1994 edition of her exhaustive study *Rock Art in Utah* Polly Schaafsma is able to add little to remarks she made in the 1971 edition that "very little is known about the pur-pose or significance" of the drawings made by one prehistoric subculture, or that for another "the significance and purpose . . . are also unclear," and for yet a third remained both "tantalizing" and "elusive" in spite of the best minds that could be put to its study. The most she can offer by way of interpretation in 1994 is this: "In the east, the Utah Tradition of rock art, in which shamanic anthropomorphic figures predominated across a number of stylistic bound-aries, suggests an on-going, powerful ideological theme embraced by the majority of eastern Utah's prehistoric people for several thousand years. Carried on into the late prehistoric period by the Fremont culture, it appears to have ended with the disappearance or waning of the Fremont between A.D. 1000 and 1300, depending on the area."

The people who are ghosts probably will keep at least some of their secrets, then. But not everything. We know, or at least can guess with some confidence, that the first inhabitants of the Southwest came to the region anywhere from twenty-five thousand to ten thousand years ago, offshoots from a series of migrations that brought the original Paleo-Indian immigrants of North and South America across the Bering Land Bridge from the Asian continent. The earliest of the southwestern settlers were the Sandia, Folsom, and Cochise cultures, groups so much more evolved than their Paleo-Indian ancestors that they are classified as "Archaic." Gatherers and hunters, these Archaic people lived in caves and other sheltered spots and depended for their livelihood on foraging for pine nuts, ricegrass, lily bulbs, sunflower seeds, and edibles from other wild plants, and on whatever they could kill with snares, spears, and bows and arrows. Within a few thousand years, the people had evolved into even more complex and sophisticated societies divided into three roughly distinct cultures called the Mogollon, the Hohokam, and the Anasazi.

The Mogollon people extended from northern Mexico into central New Mexico and east-central Arizona; the Hohokam resided west and south of the Mogollon people in the Sonoran Desert country from the Gila River and lower Colorado River valleys into northwestern Mexico. It was the Anasazi who came to dominate the Four Corners region in prehistoric time, including most of the canyon country of southern Utah, the Anasazi who left their structures in the walls and riverbeds and mesa tops of this land, their marks on the stones. Like the Archaic people, they began their time here by living in caves and natural rock shelters, relying on primitive hunting technology and constant gathering to survive. By the eighth century A.D., however, they had begun to cultivate squash and corn, make exquisitely contrived basketry, and live in gatherings of pit houses and then surface dwellings that grew increasingly more complex; they began to devise clay pots and invest their lives with a complex religious system of myths and totemism in which the kiva, a beehive-shaped structure, became each community's central place of worship. Built partly above ground and partly below ground and accessible only from a hole in its roof, the kiva apparently symbolized the belief (shared by the Hopi and other Indian people of later centuries) that it was from the underworld that the human species had first emerged.

In the middle of the ninth century rainfall increased slightly, especially during summer months, and remained above average for the next three hundred years or so. The Anasazi became very successful. They began to cluster in larger and larger communities in structures made of earth which would come to

"Indian" corn and metates, location undisclosed.

*Anasazi granaries,
location undisclosed.*

be called pueblos. Some, like the huge Chetro Ketl Pueblo in Chaco Canyon, New Mexico, grew to include as many as five hundred rooms and, with other pueblos in the canyon, comprised what could almost be called a metropolitan region, with an estimated population of five thousand. The people learned to build and use looms to weave their clothing and blankets and their pottery became more sophisticated and beautifully decorated. Walled fields of corn, squash, and beans grew to cover many acres, watered now by complex irrigation systems that collected rainfall in dammed catch-basins on the mesa tops, then channeled it down to the fields. They established trade routes and a complicated theocracy to bind their society together.

By the middle of the twelfth century, however, decline began to set in, beginning the tradition of boom and bust that would characterize the economic nature of the West from that point forward. No one yet knows precisely why. For many years, a series of prolonged droughts that began about this time was considered the major cause, though there had been equally serious dry periods in preceding centuries. Others have laid the blame on ever more savage raids from aggressive peoples like the antecedents of the Navajo and Apache, even though these people did not enter the Southwest until the middle of the fifteenth century, long after decline had already set in. Some others have pointed to the depletion of natural resources like wood or to severe erosion and silt deposition from too much irrigation, still others to the likelihood of social disintegration because of growing urban congestion and competition over resources. Most likely, the answer is pretty close to "all of the above" (leaving out the Navajos and Apaches as factors), at least according to the speculations of New Mexico anthropologist Nancy Cordell. "The actual depopulation of vast areas of the ancient Anasazi home land," she writes in Anasazi World, "was probably due to a combination of factors: more variation in summer rainfall than had occurred in the past, the depletion of wood supplies for heating and building material, and the failure of the social ties of trade, exchange, and ceremonial sharing to provide for the people's needs. With life becoming more difficult, it is likely that factional disputes broke out more often. As a result some people sought homes with relatives and friends in distant villages. Possibly, too, disputes between villages occurred over access to farmland or firewood, and, again, some of the people may have left to seek their fortunes elsewhere."

For whatever reason or combination of reasons, over many decades small pueblos began to close down, their people moving out of the canyon country. At first, the people gathered in fewer but larger pueblos, like those of Chaco

Canyon or Mesa Verde in southwestern Colorado, but in time these, too, were depopulated, until by the sixteenth century the culture that had once given the land of the Four Corners its human character had simply vanished, its people slowly retracting south and east, becoming assimilated with other, more successful Indian pueblo cultures, like those in the valley of the Rio Grande, their places taken now by Navajo and Hopi people and by descendants of the Fremont culture of the Great Basin just to the northwest – the Paiutes, Utes, and Gosiutes – who would all find their own measure of disaster in the next turn of the great wheel of history.

Under the never ending summer sun you could see them coming across the desert for miles, a clanking, irregular line of seventeen mounted men, light bouncing off their helmets and breastplates under which they must have suffered unspeakable tortures of heat and sweat. For some of them, those few who practiced flagellations and other self-inflicted torments in order to share in the redemptive pain of Christ on his dolorous walk to Calvary, this probably was an added benefit. Were they not here in this execrable land for the greater glory of God, after all? That, and a little something for King Charles of Spain and, not incidentally, themselves.

The year was 1540, and the men were members of a subsidiary expedition sent off from the main body of the greatest exploring enterprise the New World had yet seen – 230 caballeros recruited from the greedy nobility of New Spain (Mexico), with numerous footmen, 5 friars to carry the word of God, a military escort of 62 foot soldiers, 1,800 Mexican Indian and Negro servants and slaves, and 1,500 horses, mules, and beef cattle. Under the overall command of Francisco Vasquez de Coronado, the expedition had been sent out of Compostela, Mexico, by Viceroy Don Antonio de Mendoza that spring to find the Seven Cities of Cíbola, unimaginably rich enclaves where gold was so abundant that the very buildings were made of it and it was used for the most mundane of everyday objects, from utensils to chamber pots. Or so the Spaniards had it on good authority – that being their own desperate need to believe in the possibility of untold riches in this otherwise incomprehensible land, combined with various gaseous rumors, each more splendiferous than the one before, that had been floating around in the New World even before Hernán Cortés had reduced the Aztec empire to ruins less than twenty years before.

By the middle of the summer, the main expedition had found their first "city," a large pueblo occupied by Zuñi Indians in northwestern New Mexico.

Anasazi panel, location undisclosed.

Overleaf: Butler Wash Ruins behind Comb Ridge.

There was, of course, no gold to be found, and in frustration Coronado had sent out subsidiary expeditions into the land to see what could be seen. The smallest, under the command of Don Pedro de Tovar, was the force that now struggled slowly northwest toward the edge of the south rim of the Grand Canyon. Pedro de Castañeda, the Coronado expedition's official chronicler, told the story:

> After they had gone twenty days they came to the banks of the river [the Colorado]. It seemed to be more than three or four leagues in an air line across to the other bank of the stream which flowed between them. . . . They spent three days on this bank looking for a passage down to the river, which looked from above as if the water was six feet across, although the Indians said it was half a league wide. It was impossible to descend, for after these three days Captain Melgosa and one Juan Galeras and another companion, who were the three lightest and most agile men, made an attempt to go down at the least most difficult place, and went down until those above were unable to keep sight of them. They returned about four o'clock in the afternoon, not having succeeded in reaching the bottom on account of the great difficulties which they found, because what seemed to be easy from above was not so, but instead very hard and difficult. They said they had been down about a third of the way and that the river seemed very large from the place which they reached, and that from what they saw they thought the Indians had given the width correctly. Those who stayed above had estimated that some huge rocks on the sides of the cliffs seemed to be about as tall as a man, but those who went down swore that when they reached these rocks they were bigger than the great tower of Seville.

Having thus been the first Europeans to get a glimpse of deceptive and demanding reality in canyon country, Don Pedro de Tovar and his men made their way back to the main expedition and reported to Coronado that it would be useless to proceed in that direction. The expedition ultimately turned northeast, following yet another rumor, this one of a land called Gran Quivira, whose emperor slept under a tree hung with golden bells. This magical land, insisted every group of Indian people the expedition encountered, was always just ahead, merely a few easy leagues beyond the next rise of land (move on,

Granaries tucked into slickrock wall, location undisclosed.

Spaniard, move on). The search for Gran Quivira ended on the plains of Kansas, where the only discovery of note was that of the creature we now call the buffalo, and by the end of 1542 Coronado and his men were back in Mexico City with nothing to show for their efforts but a great deal of experience traveling around in a land they could not begin to comprehend. No European would venture into canyon country again for another 234 years.

The Spanish had effectively subdued the various Pueblo people who inhabited the valley of the Rio Grande in New Mexico by then, had established their own thriving urban center at Santa Fe, and were well on the way toward doing the same in California, where in 1776 a nascent settlement had been established at Monterey. It was a long sea journey to Monterey from Mexican ports on the Gulf of California, however, and the "land bridge" to California from northwestern Mexico was always in danger of being cut off by hostile Indians. Why not find another route directly from Santa Fe? That, at least, was the dream of Father Francisco Silvestre Velez de Escalante, a priest who on July 29, 1776, set off in marvelous ignorance with eight other men, including the alcalde, or mayor, of Santa Fe. They traveled northwest up the valley of the Chama River, crossed the San Juan River, then headed northwest to the Dolores River, crossed it, continued north to the Colorado River, fording it near present-day Grand Junction, Colorado, moved on to the White River, then turned west into Utah, crossing the Wasatch Range and wandering down the long valley of the Great Salt Lake to Utah Lake, where they arrived early in October. They were nearly starving by now, and the tops of the mountains they could see all around them were covered by snow. They decided they could never get across the Great Basin to the Sierra Nevada before winter closed down all the passes, so they turned in a southeasterly direction and headed back, they hoped, to Santa Fe.

Already an ambitious undertaking, the expedition now became an epic journey of survival, the men staggering straight into the canyon country of south-central Utah, surrounded, as Escalante later desribed it, "by mesas and inaccessible heights," picking their way up steep canyons and over "perilous ledges of rock," through storms "with horrible thunder and lightning" during which they "chanted the Litany of the Virgin in order that She might ask some relief for [them]," foraging for pine nuts, herbs, and roots, increasingly exhausted and desperate. They crossed the Virgin River, moved down to the Kanab Plateau in northwest Arizona, then turned east, just missing seeing the Grand Canyon from the north rim. By the time they reached the Colorado River again at a point above Lee's Ferry, they were eating their horses. It was a place they had

66

to cross, they believed, if they were not to be lost forever in the canyons. They cut steps into the face of the cliffs in order to get the remaining horses down to the river, then hesitated, watching the wide, fast-flowing stretch of water nervously. Finally, Escalante wrote, "One of the men waded in and found it good, not having to swim at any place. We followed him on horseback a little lower down, and when halfway across, two horses which went ahead lost their footing and swam a short distance. We waited, although in some peril, until the first wader returned from the other side to guide us and then we crossed with ease." By about five o'clock in the afternoon of November 7, all the men were safely across the river, "praising God our Lord and firing off a few muskets as a sign of the great joy which we all felt at having overcome so great a difficulty and which had cost us so much labor and delay. . . ." The Crossing of the Fathers, as it would be called, was the last major barrier between them and the final leg of the journey back to Santa Fe. Escalante's trek was the second, and last, expression of Spanish empire in the canyon country, and it would be nearly seventy-five years before Europeans or their descendants ventured here again.

Until the end of the 1840s, the land of stone time remained the nearly unchallenged fiefdom of the Ute Indians, who not only dominated the northern and central regions of Utah but kept the poorer and less socially organized Paiutes to the south in fear of their lives. Not even the otherwise indefatigable mountain men made significant forays into the region during the height of the brief, if colorful and (to beavers) devastating fur trade industry during the decades of the 1820s and 1830s. The United States would not take official title to the region until after the successful conclusion of what can best be described as our only unabashed war of territorial conquest, the Mexican War of 1846–1848. We had wanted California, and got it; but with it came just about everything between the Missouri River and the Mexican border. Which is not to say that we knew quite what to do with much of it, especially that portion that lay between South Pass in Wyoming and the Grand Canyon in Arizona. For a while, it was just country we needed to cross in order to get to someplace else – Oregon and California, mainly, where dreams of Manifest Destiny (and later, gold) beckoned.

Then came the most extraordinary collection of pioneers in American history, the members of the Church of Jesus Christ of Latter-Day Saints, also known as the Mormons, and, to themselves, the Saints. Because of their doctrine of polygamy (not officially ended by the church until 1891) and their own proud clannishness, the Mormons had been driven, often violently, from whatever enclaves they had tried to settle east of the Mississippi River. Under the leadership of Brigham Young, they finally moved en masse to the valley of the Great Salt Lake in 1847 and proceeded to build what they called the State of Deseret, the most successful venture in cooperative social engineering in American history and the only functioning theocracy since the days of the Puritans. The United States government, in fact, finally had to resort to armed intervention in the "Mormon War" of 1858 to establish once and for all the jurisdiction of the federal government over the Mormon hegemony – but even after that exercise in realpolitik, the church continued to enjoy tremendous control over nearly every aspect of the region's life, from the policies and programs of its territorial and (after 1896) state governments to the shape of its industrial development and social habits. It still does.

Meanwhile, constantly seeking to expand the church's territory and influence, Young sent colonizers out from Salt Lake City to all the points of the western compass, from southern Idaho to northern Arizona, western Nevada to southern California, where the villages sprouted, each surrounded by irrigated farm fields, each laid out according to the neat, spacious, wide-streeted, divinely-ordained plats that had been handed down to the settlers by their founder, Joseph Smith, each a celebration of green. "Because Mormon colonization was group colonization," Wallace Stegner wrote in *Mormon Country*, "and because the family was and is of tremendous importance in the social structure of the Saints, and because the women of those families insisted (and would have insisted even if Brigham Young had not actively promoted the practice) on carrying rose cuttings and geranium slips and flower seeds and seedling trees across more than a thousand miles of wilderness, the Mormon village is a green village. The Gentiles who had driven the Saints from Ohio and Missouri and Illinois were contemptuous both of the Mormons and the arid desert they had settled upon. It was necessary to love these valleys . . . as the fairest land on earth, because they were sanctuary. And it was unthinkable that the gathering-place of the Saints should be a barren desert. It should be made to blossom, and it was." As early as the mid-1850s, the green villages of the Saints had begun to sprout even in central and southern Utah, in places that were among the least hospitable to traditional American settlement of any on earth, pockets, as Stegner wrote, where "settlements are literally hewn out of the rock, founded with incredible labor and sustained against conditions that would have driven out a less persistent people after one year." Against all odds, the unstoppable Saints gradually displaced even the powerful Utes,

Anasazi ruin, location undisclosed.

Modern ruin by the
roadside near Hanksville.

building tiny green islands surrounded by all the red-walled wilderness of stone – Moab and Manti, St. George and Kanab, Loa and Castle Dale, Huntington and Fremont, a dozen more – building each according to Saintly dictates, passing on from one generation to the next the implacable but comforting rituals of Mormon community and religion.

The land might have survived such a hard-won compromise between ambition and reality largely intact had circumstances not begun to change; even today, the old Mormon towns, farms, and ranches in the Castle Valley, for example, seem to have grown little beyond what the land can sustain comfortably – on the surface, at least. But it was not in the nature of western development that things should remain in a condition of stasis, even in Utah. Here as elsewhere, development would be the province of the boomers in whose fevered imaginations there were few or no limits to what the land could support. Should there be a metropolis for every valley, surrounded by farms the size of small European countries, industrial ranching enterprises stretching from horizon to horizon, every riverbed exposed and dredged for gold, mining holes drilled and dynamited into every promising mountainside, ancient sediments mercilessly gouged for coal and punctured for oil, every stream dammed to provide water wherever water was wanted, the land made to give up all that the dreams promised? Of course, and never mind what rationality might have to say.

The land of stone time was prey to at least some of this unbridled enthusiasm, though less than other parts of the West or the state. A few offshoots of the gold and silver mining excitements that had punctuated the West since 1849 sprang up here in the 1870s and 1880s, giving birth to a few transient mining camps like Silver Reef west of Zion – although the nearest thing to genuine paydirt in the region came in the form of coal in the northern portions of the Castle Valley near Price and iron in the high country over near Cedar City, together with a little potash here and there. Timber operations on the Aquarius Plateau began skinning off significant amounts of the original ponderosa pine forest on Boulder Mountain, hauling it down to mills in Escalante and other towns. A network of highways laced through the redrock and crossed the rivers.

This steady if less than spectacular development, enlivened somewhat by a growing tourist industry, continued well into the twentieth century before being interrupted, briefly but resoundingly, by the great uranium rush of the 1950s. This twentieth-century version of the California gold rush sent prospectors, speculators, corporate geologists, con artists, and crooks into every nook

Paved section of Burr Trail through Long Canyon.

and cranny of the red-walled country, transforming little Moab and other sleepy communities into glittering atomic cities, and investing most of southern Utah with an unaccustomed frenzy before this boom, like all booms, died away, leaving a handful of functioning mines, a couple of uranium refining plants, numerous ghost towns and abandoned mines, and even more disappointment in its wake. Reeling slightly, the region returned to the steady exploitation of its natural resources and the development of the tourist industry, its population growing in both numbers and diversity now but still lagging behind the explosive, almost uncontrolled growth experienced down the Wasatch Front, as Salt Lake City and its sister cities inexorably merged into one enormous urban and industrial clot.

So far, it is the rivers of the region that have suffered the greatest change in canyon country. This is not the fault of Major John Wesley Powell. The major (as he was known to one and all) had earned his rank during the Civil War, and at the Battle of Shiloh had lost his right arm, a condition that did not slow him down measurably. A largely self-taught naturalist, geologist, and ethnologist, Powell went on to organize and lead some of the most important exploring expeditions since the days of Lewis and Clark. Chief among these were his surveys of the Colorado Plateau region, during the first of which he and a crew of ten adventurers had climbed into wooden boats at Green River, Wyoming, in May 1869, and set off on one of the great river journeys of history down the Green and Colorado rivers and through the Grand Canyon, surviving house-sized rapids, frequent wrecks, and ever-diminishing rations, though three of the river-runners would be killed by Indians after the journey. Powell went on to write a best-seller about the trip, *Exploration of the Colorado River of the West and Its Tributaries*, published in 1875. More importantly, his newfound fame enabled him to persuade Congress to support a major survey of the entire Plateau Province.

From 1871 to 1878, with the major himself departing and rejoining the survey team periodically, with personnel additions and changes, and with continuing financial support, the geographical and geological survey of the Plateau Province would map the canyons and rivers and outline the geological history of the region, tramp across mountains and run rivers, delve into the ethnology of the native population, take hundreds of photographs, and produce an intellectual treasure trove of raw data that would enable the survey's scientists to illuminate for the first time the complicated landforms in this immense territory and to formulate many definitions and explanations whose validity has remained essentially unchallenged to this day. Two major publications emerged

Graveyard near Torrey.

Temple of the
Church of Jesus Christ of
Latter-Day Saints, Manti.

from these years, too. Clarence E. Dutton's *Tertiary History of the Grand Canyon District* (1882) was both an intrepid scholarly study and a remarkably literate, even poetic, description of the origins and character of canyon country. Powell's own effort, more mundane as literature than Dutton's work, nevertheless was even more significant as analysis. Published in 1878, his *Report on the Lands of the Arid Region of the United States* punctured immediately one of the fondest visions of the boomers, the notion that the West, like the eastern third of the nation, could be made to support not only thriving metropolises but millions of small independent farms where descendants of Jefferson's virtuous yeomen, the very core of the democratic idea, would raise up families and enrich themselves, their regions, and their country. Once the westward movement had crossed the Mississippi into the Great Plains, the dream found articulation in the Homestead Act of 1862, which guaranteed to the presumed yeoman at least 160 acres of the public domainon which to carve out his little corner of Eden. Eden, however, began to deteriorate the farther west one went; there simply was too much land and too little water.

Never mind, the boomers said; irrigation was the answer. Irrigate, and all the billions of acres west of the Mississippi would blossom as the rose. Couldn't be done, Powell said in his 1878 report: "Within the Arid Region," he wrote with devastating simplicity, "only a small portion of the country is irrigable." The boomers refused to listen, as boomers will. During the 1890s, "irrigation congresses" began to convene regularly, calling for the government to step in to build irrigation works in the West that would provide the water for "a million forty-acre farms." The 1893 congress, held in Salt Lake City, invited the major to speak. Bad idea. Powell had not changed his mind since 1878; if anything, he had grown even more certain that the dreams were not going to work in the arid West. "I wish to make it clear to you," he told them, "there is not enough water to irrigate all these lands; there is not sufficient water to irrigate all the lands that could be irrigated, and only a small portion can be irrigated. . . . I tell you, gentlemen, you are piling up a heritage of conflict . . . for there is not sufficient water to supply the land!" Still, the boomers would not listen. In 1902, they persuaded Congress to pass the Newlands Act, creating the Reclamation Service (later to become the Bureau of Reclamation). Powell had warned that even where irrigation was possible the scarcity of water could lead to monopoly ("The question," he said in the arid regions report, "is to devise some practical means by which water rights may be distributed among individual farmers and water monopolies prevented"). The act attempted to address that question by stipulating that anyone receiving water from a federally sponsored irrigation project was limited to 160 acres of land irrigated by that water. The 160-acre limitation, fought bitterly by western agribusiness interests from the moment it went into effect, never was enforced with any consistency, and so the myth of the great garden in the West filled with a million forty-acre farms withered and died, replaced by factories in the fields and wandering armies of migrant laborers.

In the meantime, armed with federal money and federal water contracts, the U. S. Bureau of Reclamation proceeded to build the greatest water works projects in the history of humankind. Among the earliest and by far the most ambitious were those contructed for the Colorado River Basin, beginning with Boulder (later Hoover) Dam on the Lower Colorado, completed in 1936 and behind which there soon appeared the region's first major artificial body of water — Lake Mead. Soon after, came Parker Dam and Lake Havasu a few miles to the south, then Imperial Dam, then Davis Dam, then the Palo Verde Diversion Dam, then the Headgate Rock Diversion Dam, and, finally, down in Mexico, Morelos Dam and reservoir. Most years now, the wild Colorado — the river the engineers themselves called "Big Red," the river whose passage through the great uplift of the Colorado Plateau had shaped the very land — this great river no longer even made it all the way to the Gulf of California, dribbling down to a fetid green trickle and finally disappearing into the sand miles above the gulf that it once had nourished.

The engineers were not done. When conservationists rose up in the early 1950s to keep the Bureau of Reclamation from damming the Green and Yampa rivers in the middle of Dinosaur National Monument, the agency was given Glen Canyon on the Colorado as a substitute. In 1965, the bureau completed Glen Canyon Dam, and the waters slowly began to back up to form Lake Powell, flooding some of the most glorious canyon complexes on the entire Colorado Plateau, including several, like Cathedral in the Desert, through which John Wesley Powell, after whom the lake was named, had floated in 1869; the irony would not have been lost on the major. Most of the Colorado's biggest tributaries were similarly graced with big and little dams. The Green River, for example, may have missed being dammed in Dinosaur National Monument, but two big dams were constructed on its upper stem at Flaming Gorge and Fontanelle, and the Colorado River itself was threatened again in the late 1960s when the Bureau of Reclamation began to lust after dams in Bridge Canyon and Marble Canyon that would have converted more than 90 percent of the river's flow through Grand Canyon National Park to a narrow, twisting lake, not unlike Lake Powell. Once again, the conservationists took to the streets, figuratively speaking, and the dams were defeated, as they had been in Dinosaur National Monument.

But we are perhaps a more stubborn branch of the human species than those first irrigation engineers, the Anasazi, and we will not stop our dreaming. It is not in the nature of engineers to destroy plans once made, and somewhere in file drawers grown dusty with disuse, the Marble Canyon and Bridge Canyon blueprints almost certainly still reside. In the meantime, there is one major tributary of the Colorado that still flows more or less free. It is the Virgin River, whose tumbling waters are a temptation that is proving irresistible to a new set of boomers. The growth-minded residents of St. George, Utah, would like to get a big portion of the river's flow to nourish expansion plans that would allow this city of less than 20,000 to bloat, they insist, to a population of a quarter of a million people by the year 2020. The Las Vegas Valley Water District, on the other hand, wants some of it for the expansive visions of its own city; already percolating along at nearly a million people, the neon wonder in the desert expects to add nearly another million by 2030 – and to what better use, the city wants to know, could the Virgin's water conceivably be put than to fill the bellies and swimming pools of all these people? Other communities and enterprises express similar longings, and the state of Utah has seriously identified as many as sixteen sites where the river might be dammed to the profit of any number of them.

However, the days when growth could still be passed off as an unqualified good without serious contradiction are gone, even in canyon country. Here, as elsewhere in the state and the nation, there is a powerful opposition to the notion of damming the Virgin River, and the boomers already have found it almost impossible to have their way with this river, as their ancestors did with the Colorado. Their petitions are questioned, challenged, sometimes blocked, and even the Bureau of Reclamation has been dancing nervously around the question of adding the Virgin to its waterworks collection. The Virgin almost certainly will survive, because the rivers of southern Utah, like the wonderlands they have created, have become the focus of something new – a widespread and growing movement that would preserve, finally and as close to forever as human dreams ever get, the last of the wildness in the land of stone time.

Abandoned truck body, Reds Canyon, San Rafael Swell.

Above: Looking toward the rim-rock of Sam's Mesa above the Dirty Devil River. Left: Storm clouds over Tarantuala Mesa and the Strike Valley. Right: Upper Calf Creek Falls, Escalante River canyons.

Overleaf: Monolith in Arch Canyon.

STONE TIME

Mesa top and house-sized boulders near
Coal Mine Wash, San Rafael Swell.

82

Part IV: Remnants

In March 30, 1935, the last bucket of concrete that went into the great curving wall of what was then still called Boulder Dam skimmed out over the top of the 726-foot structure, stopped, then dumped its viscous load into the last empty form. The greatest engineering feat of its day was now effectively done, the Colorado River plugged, its ancient task of carrying the land of the Colorado Plateau to the sea interrupted – at least until such time as Lake Mead behind the dam finally is filled with silt and the river is able to return to its own engineering job. Less than three months before the final load of concrete spilled out of its bucket, a group of men had gathered at the Cosmos Club in Washington, D.C. – a club, as it happened, of which Major John Wesley Powell had been a co-founder – and put their names to the articles of incorporation of an organization that would dedicate itself to the preservation of the American wilderness and the prevention of just such outsized expressions of misdirected progress as Boulder Dam.

The organization, logically enough, called itself The Wilderness Society, and while its numbers would not reach even a thousand until well after World War II, its single-minded dedication to the wilderness idea helped make it effective far beyond its numbers. Another factor was the philosophical rightness of the idea itself, one given its greatest weight and most precise articulation by one of The Society's founders, Aldo Leopold, who saw in the preservation of wild country the most profound expression of the proper human place in the natural world. It had been Leopold, in fact, who in 1924 had persuaded the Forest Service, for which he then worked, to establish the Gila Primitive Area in New Mexico – a drive of only a few hours from the canyon country of southern Utah, coincidentally – as the first administratively designated wilderness area in the federal public lands system. In the years since that decision, the former ranger had refined his thinking on the subject of wilderness into a coherent vision that was included in his most important work, *A Sand*

Willow trees along the Dirty Devil River.

County Almanac and *Sketches Here and There* in 1949. Land, in America as elsewhere, he concluded, had been regarded as little more than a commodity in the affairs of humankind, something to be used and, if necessary, used up in the pursuit of the main chance. With the land itself lying in ruin or near ruin all around us, with wilderness and all that it could offer us vanishing beneath the plow or the pavement, it was time to take another look at ourselves in relation to the land, time to predicate a moral universe that would include the needs of the land in its system of values. He called this concept the "land ethic," and it lies at the heart of *A Sand County Almanac.* "All ethics so far evolved," he wrote, "rest upon a single premise: that the individual is a member of a community of interdependent parts. His instincts prompt him to compete for his place in that community, but his ethics prompt him also to cooperate. . . . The land ethic simply enlarges the boundaries of the community to include soils, waters, plants, and animals, or collectively, the land. . . . In short, a land ethic changes the role of Homo sapiens from conqueror of the land-community to plain member and citizen of it. It implies respect for his fellow-members and also respect for the community as such."

Armed with Leopold's idea, if not with Leopold himself (he died in 1948 without ever seeing the published version of *A Sand County Almanac*), The Wilderness Society, in league now with the Sierra Club, the Izaak Walton League, the National Audubon Society, and other activist lights of the growing conservation movement, turned to the task of institutionalizing the land ethic's most important protocol: the preservation of the wild. After the successful defense of Dinosaur National Monument in the mid-1950s, the movement's leaders concluded that it was no longer enough to run to the protection of every wild area that might be threatened with development of one kind or another; what was needed was a process by which such areas would be placed under protection long before being imperiled directly. The result was the Wilderness Act, legislation first introduced to Congress in 1956 and reintroduced, revised, debated, mutilated, patched back together, and finally passed in the summer of 1964. On September 3, 1964, President Lyndon Johnson signed the act and made it law. It now was, as the act's preamble stated, "the policy of the Congress to secure for the American people of present and future generations the benefits of an enduring resource of wilderness. For this purpose there is hereby established a National Wilderness Preservation System to be composed of federally owned areas designated by Congress as 'wilderness areas,' and these shall be administered for the use and enjoyment of the American people in such manner and by such means as will leave them unimpaired. . . . A wilderness, in contrast with those areas where man and his own works dominate the landscape, is hereby recognized as an area where the earth and its community of life are untrammeled by man, where man himself is a visitor who does not remain."

The act immediately established the beginnings of the National Wilderness Preservation System by designating 9.1 million acres of official wilderness in national forest areas (including Leopold's Gila Primitive Area) that already had been administratively identified by the Forest Service as essentially wild. The rest would have to come after each of the federal land-managing agencies surveyed their territory and recommended to Congress which areas qualified as candidates for wilderness designation, and Congress passed the appropriate legislation. Slowly, year by year, acre by acre, agency by agency, state by state, bill by painstakingly crafted bill, almost always with controversy, sometimes with near-violent conflict, like that over the 56 million acres of wilderness included in the Alaska Lands Act of 1980, the system grew. Today, it includes nearly 600 individual wilderness areas in a little under 100 million acres of the 634 million acres embraced in the national parks, national forests, national wildlife refuges, and lands of the Bureau of Land Management. It is a legacy of wild country enjoyed by no other people on the planet.

I have gone on at such length about the Wilderness Act of 1964 not only because the conservation community and the government are preparing to celebrate the 30th anniversary of the act even as I write, but because of the fact that of all the hundreds of wilderness areas that have been designated over the past thirty years, only fifteen are in Utah, and only three in the heart of the land of stone time itself — Dark Canyon in Manti-La Sal National Forest, Box-Death Hollow in Dixie National Forest, and Paria Canyon-Vermillion Cliffs on a piece of BLM land in northern Arizona that juts into southern Utah above the Colorado River.

The reasons for all the blank areas on the wilderness map of southern Utah are instructive, if a little depressing. First, many of the longtime residents of the state and region, especially those with stakes in an economic tradition that is devoted to the extraction of minerals and timber and the production of cattle and cattle feed, have always had difficulty accepting the fact that the federal government (which is to say, the American people as a whole) owns so much territory within their state and have consistently fought against any kind of regulation that might hinder them in the pursuit of what they can get out of the land. These were the kinds of citizens, handsomely supported by the state's congressional delegation, who bitterly resisted the proposal first put forth by Interior Secretary Harold L. Ickes in 1936 that most of the canyon country of southern Utah be folded into a 4.4 million-acre federal reserve called Escalante National Monument. Those in the state who wanted to protect anything at all had considered a national park unit of, say, 35,000 acres or so along the Colorado River to be acceptable. The Escalante proposal exploded among them like an artillery shell fired from the enemy's stronghold in Washington, D.C., and before the smoke cleared the government had to settle for the 241,904-acre compromise that became Capitol Reef National Monument (upgraded to a national park in 1971). The only other major chunk of federally-protected land that survived Ickes's original proposal was Canyonlands National Park, and it was not established until 1964. As that delay suggests, not all that much has changed since the 1930s. The generation of Utahns who fought Ickes in the heart of the Great Depression would have no trouble applauding the sentiments of William Howell, executive director of the Southeastern Utah Association of Local Governments in 1987. "I do want to preserve our natural environment for posterity," Howell wrote in Stewart Aitchison's book *Utah Wildlands*, "but I have seen the avaricious behavior of some environmental groups and government agencies which rivals the rapacious acts of early land despoilers and rides roughshod over the rights of local residents. I have seen the livelihood of people curtailed and the economy of a local area strangled by those groups."

Second, most of the land that needs and deserves protection as wilderness in southern Utah is under the administrative aegis of the Bureau of Land Management, probably the federal land agency least admired among environmentalists (the regard has been mutual, for the most part). The BLM, a bureaucratic amalgam contrived in 1946 out of the General Land Office and the Grazing Service, holds administrative title to about 236 million acres of public land, a little over 22 million of them in Utah. Almost devoid of any readily perceived identity as a land-protection agency, much less any coherence of purpose and vision, the BLM soon became so supportive of various extractive industries that irreverent conservationists dubbed it the "Bureau of Livestock and Mining." In its defense (sort of), for thirty years the agency was not compelled to even consider such things as wilderness protection, not even by the Wilderness Act of 1964; one of the many compromises that attended passage of the act was a provision that exempted the BLM from its provisions. Wilderness was not in the bureau's charter, and any protection it happened to provide, as in the designation of various recreational or scenic areas, was done

Cottonwood and Escalante Arch, Escalante River canyons.

Tomsich Butte, Reds Canyon, San Rafael Swell.

*Overleaf: Looking toward the Henry Mountains
across Capitol Reef National Park.*

almost entirely at its own discretion (and could be rescinded just as casually).

That state of affairs ended in 1976 with passage of the Federal Land Policy and Management Act (FLPMA). The act directed the BLM to make an inventory of all its roadless and otherwise undeveloped lands and determine which had potential as additions to the National Wilderness Preservation System. While the inventory continued, all the lands under study were to be protected from any new development and once those areas that might qualify as wilderness were identified, they were to be set aside as Wilderness Study Areas (WSAs) and kept inviolate until Congress decided which should be included in the wilderness system.

In Utah, as in most other western states, the BLM moved with glacial reluctance to satisfy the requirements of the law. Nevertheless, early in 1986, nearly ten years after FLPMA, the Utah BLM issued the draft form of its *Statewide Wilderness Environmental Impact Statement*. In the statement, the agency's wilderness review team identified 3.2 million acres out of its total holdings in Utah of 22 million that qualified for study as wilderness areas. Of those 3.2 million acres, the bureau recommended a little under 1.9 million for wilderness designation. Gregory Thayn, the team leader for the study process, attempted to explain why the draft statement was received a little coldly by the conservation community. "The subjective nature of the wording in the definition of wilderness in the Wilderness Act of 1964 (i.e., 'substantially' unnoticable imprint of man, 'outstanding' opportunities for solitude or a primitive and unconfined type of recreation), and the requirement for weighing wilderness values against other potential resource uses has led the BLM wilderness process into controversy with wilderness proponents and opponents who take issue with the BLM's judgment and recommendations."

That was putting it mildly. The fact was, conservationists detected in the draft Environmental Impact Statement a profound determination on the part of the BLM's Utah team to come up with any fragile reason that would enable it to leave out of wilderness consideration everything it possibly could. One means by which this was accomplished was by interpreting the definition of valid wilderness with great rigidity, while at the same time accepting even rumor as being sufficient evidence to identify potential economic benefits in any given area that would be "lost" to development if the area were designated wilderness. The results were sometimes so ludicrous they astonished even

Beaver dam on the Escalante River.

BLM officials. Terry Sopher, then director of the BLM's wilderness program in Washington, D.C., went out to take a look at what the agency's people were up to in Utah in 1980 and later called most of what he had witnessed "absurd." At one point, for example, he had been flown over Labyrinth Canyon on the Green River where "you were looking down on the ground, and one side of the river was said to have outstanding characteristics and the other side was said not to have, and they both looked identical. . . . Based on what we had seen, there was an egregious violation of the policies." There was a great deal of that sort of thing going on in canyon country, Sopher concluded. He returned to Washington and recommended to the bureau's director, Frank Gregg, that the Utah wilderness inventory be scrapped and its team ordered to start over. Before Gregg could make any such move, Ronald Reagan took office, James Gaius Watt became secretary of the interior, Gregg (a Carter appointee) was dismissed, Robert Burford put in his place, and in Utah as elsewhere the BLM's wilderness review teams were allowed – indeed, encouraged – to misinterpret the law however they conveniently chose to do so. Sopher went to work for The Wilderness Society.

Both The Wilderness Society and the Sierra Club had an active presence in Utah by the time the BLM's preposterous draft statement on wilderness was released in 1986, but the greatest and most knowledgeable local opposition to the agency's conclusions came from a growing collection of grassroots organizations. Chief among these was the Southern Utah Wilderness Alliance, founded in 1983 by another disgruntled former BLM employee, Clive Kincaid, and a handful of like-minded folk and dedicated to the principle that whatever the BLM might admit was worthy of protection in Utah, the chances were excellent that at least twice as much, probably more, actually deserved it. Under Kincaid, then Brant Calkin, and now Mike Matz as its executive directors (conservation activism in Utah has a large burnout potential), the organization has grown to nearly ten thousand members, some 20 percent of whom are Utahns. But even in the beginning SUWA operated as if it were one of the so-called "fat-cat" environmental monsters that conservatives see lurking in Washington, D.C., or San Francisco, not only proceeding to challenge the BLM's wilderness study process but taking it and the Forest Service on with energy and expertise over such management practices as "range conversion," whereby juniper and piñon pine forests are removed by dragging huge chains across the landscape so that the land can be planted in grasses that cows like to eat, together with a numbing variety of other issues. SUWA fought attempts on the part of Garfield County to pave the Burr Trail, a scenic dirt road that wound through the country of the

Escalante River to Capitol Reef National Park, and finally lost. It fought to keep a genuine highway from being rammed through the Book Cliffs, and finally won. It fought to get cows out of the drainage of the habitat-rich Comb Wash Grazing Allotment, and finally won. It fought the Forest Service over a decision to lease sensitive areas on the south side of the Abajo Mountains in Manti-La Sal National Forest to oil and gas development, and finally won. It fought, and continues to fight, to keep roads out of wilderness study areas, oil drills out of potential wilderness, cows out of riparian areas, intrusive helicopter flights out of the wild country around Moab, off-road vehicles out of places where they have no business being, dams out of the Virgin River drainage, clear-cutting timber operations out of the steadily vanishing ponderosa pine forests of Boulder Mountain in Dixie National Forest. . . .

And so on, with a lot of help from its friends. But perhaps SUWA's most significant contribution has been to form and then help lead a collection of local and national conservation and other interested groups in an organization called the Utah Wilderness Coalition. The UWC was created late in 1984 and in February 1985 held the first of many meetings over the question of the BLM's paltry wilderness recommendations in Utah. There was more that needed preservation, all were agreed, and the UWC was determined to prove it. To that end, the organization sent volunteers out into the land like so many Mormon missionaries. "We know what's out there," SUWA board member and Wilderness Society staffer Darrell Knuffke said. "It's wilderness. And we intend to do everything in our power to keep it that way." After nearly two years of intensive exploration, what the UWC's volunteer wilderness inventory team had discovered was printed up, neatly and with style, in a huge report called *Wilderness at the Edge: A Citizen Proposal to Protect Utah's Canyons and Deserts.* Published in 1987, with an introduction by Wallace Stegner and major contributions from writer and photographer Ray Wheeler and others, *Wilderness at the Edge* used photographs, maps, and exquisitely detailed descriptions to offer up a treasure of more than 5 million acres of potential additions to the National Wilderness Preservation System. Some of the discoveries were in the "West Desert" region of the state on the edge of the Great Basin, but most were in the land of stone time: the Dirty Devil River canyons, Comb Ridge, *both* sides of Labyrinth Canyon, the Escalante canyons, Hondoo country, the Kaiparowits Plateau, the Book Cliffs, the Henry Mountains, the San Rafael Reef, Nokai Dome, Muddy Creek, the Mussentuchit Bad lands, Factory Butte — in all, 168 units of wild country that the BLM either had overlooked entirely or had badly shorted even when it did include them.

The BLM's Utah team reacted to the notion that there might be 5.1 million acres of wilderness potential in Utah with disdain, as expected. Apparently unconcerned, the team put the final touches on its own recommendations, adding only 80,000 acres to its original proposals, passed it on to its superiors, and, in effect, closed the file. Utah Congressman Wayne Owens, who at the time may have been the only elected activist conservationist in the entire state, was more receptive to the UWC discoveries. So receptive, in fact, that in 1988 he introduced H.R. 1500, the Utah Wilderness Bill, basing it on the coalition's proposals. As expected, the legislation was violently opposed by the rest of the state's congressional delegation, as well as its governor and its legislature, and consequently was mired in a legislative bog. But it could not be ignored, because SUWA, the UWC, The Wilderness Society, and any number of other folk were not about to let it be ignored. The original H.R. 1500 still lurked in the swamps of Washington when Owens was defeated in an attempt to win a Senate seat in 1992. The legislative banner was then raised by Congressman Maurice Hinchey of Massachusetts, who reintroduced the bill – expanded now to include 5.7 million acres – in 1993 and prepared to do battle for its passage, knowing full well how much effort and education it was going to take before the rest of Congress, most certainly the Utah delegation, would be willing to heed Wallace Stegner's words of admonition in the introduction to *Wilderness at the Edge:*

> The conflict in the Colorado Plateau and out in the Great Basin desert comes down to a conflict between the material and the spiritual. With only a minor and temporary sacrifice of material profit, the spiritual can be saved intact. But the attempt to generate maximum immediate profit to individuals or corporations will destroy the spiritual integrity of the wilderness.
>
> Brigham Young told his people, made restless by the California Gold Rush, to forget about gold; gold was for paving streets. If he were alive now, he might tell them that uranium is for blowing up the world, not helping it; that coal is for increasing the greenhouse effect and poisoning the world's air; that electric power is for lighting the gaming rooms and whorehouses of Las Vegas. Wilderness is for something else.
>
> The Utah deserts and plateaus and canyons are not a country of big returns, but a country of spiritual healing, incomparable for contemplation, meditation, solitude, quiet, awe, peace of mind and body. We were born of wilderness, and we respond to it more than we sometimes realize. We depend upon it increasingly for relief from the termite life we have created.

Book Cliffs at Thompson Canyon.

*Slickrock overhang in
Phipps-Death Hollow, Escalante canyons.*

*Overleaf: View from the Wedge
overlooking the San Rafael River canyons.*

Factories, power plants, resorts we can make anywhere. Wilderness, once we have given it up, is beyond our reconstruction.

So that is where protection for the land of stone time now resides. And my own explorations of discovery? They continue, will always continue. I have experienced much of this land over the past several years, but there is too little I do not know yet, too much that I have not seen. I need to get back to the San Rafael Swell, crawl into the notched magnificence in the upper reaches of Muddy Creek. I need to hold in my fist sand from the bottom of Dark Canyon. I need to watch the sun rise over the rimrock of White Canyon. I need to walk Mancos Mesa. I need to lose myself in the side canyons of the Gulch. I need to float the San Juan River, hike the Cheesebox Canyon on the edge of Natural Bridges National Monument, ford Bullfrog Creek and pull myself up to the top of Deer Creek Canyon in the Escalante Country, cross the Henry Mountains, wander in the John Henry and Warm Creek canyons of the Kaiparowits Plateau, track the roadless solitude of Fiftymile Mountain, yes, and return to all the places I have learned, though not well enough, and through all this untrammeled country seek those connections with the wild that give me, as they give all of us when we let them, the shock of recognition that reminds us of where we truly came from and who we truly are.

"Serious writers about the West," Wallace Stegner once wrote, "have often had to celebrate the scenery for the lack of the social complexities out of which most fiction is made. Geography, at least, is one matter in which a Westerner can excel and in which he takes pride. History is another." Some modern western writers of fiction — Richard Ford, say, or James Welch, Rudolfo Anaya, Leslie Marmon Silko, John Nichols, or Pam Houston — might argue that complexity is human and therefore discoverable in any community, from the hogans of a Navajo village to the boarded-up storefronts of a western boom town gone bust. And anyone familiar with novels like *The Big Rock Candy Mountain* or *Recapitulation* or any number of his short stories knows that Stegner himself had little trouble finding strands of intricacy in the western experience out of which to weave his own fiction.

Still, what he said about history and scenery cannot be usefully argued. Certainly not by me. I have written enough fiction by now to know that I probably have no business writing fiction. But I have found my own western venue in non-fiction, and with respect to me, at least, Stegner was utterly correct. While I occasionally have swerved off into other paths — most notably, New Deal and Depression history — most of the materials of a writing career that is now staggering toward its thirtieth year have been found in the western land and in the long, crowded, glorious, and despicable story of the human relationship to that land. I have written histories of California, of the Colorado River, of the spectacular mining booms that chewed their way through the landscape of the nineteenth and early twentieth century West, and of the public lands system, which in many respects *is* the story of the western landscape. I have written biographies of John Muir and Harold Ickes, who did much, each in his own way, to preserve what remained of uncorrupted land in the West. And in my work as an editor and free-lance writer, I have spent the bulk of my adult life taking on the mavens of plunder who would strip the West of its resources and leave its people impoverished. When I have not been engaged in history or informed polemic – though "advocacy journalism" is the preferred euphemism – I have been trying to discover and describe the character of the land itself, as well as the wondrous diversity of life contained within it.

This is natural enough. The writer should write, they say, about what he knows, or at least thinks he knows. Yet I suspect that something else has been going on here, too. In *Storyteller*, Pueblo Indian writer Leslie Marmon Silko writes of the ancestral tales she had heard all her young life from her Aunt Susie in the Laguna Pueblo of New Mexico, and of how those stories not only gave her a sense of the durability and richness of the Pueblo culture into which she had been born, but invested the land and the wild creatures around her with a mystical intimacy. On her horse Joey, she would ride by herself out into wild country. "I was never afraid," she writes, "[because] I carried with me the feeling I'd acquired from listening to the old stories, that the land all around me was teeming with creatures that were related to human beings and to me. The stories had also left me with a feeling of familiarity and warmth for the mesas and hills and boulders where the incidents or actions in the stories had taken place."

Like many writers about the West, I think, I have in my white-eyes fashion been trying to find in the history of my own culture's relationship to the land that same level of comfort and understanding. And I believe we are driven to do this largely because we are responding to a vestige of our own nearly forgotten past; in the western landscape, as in no other place left on the continent, we still can experience what I call the shock of recognition. In *Beyond Geography*, Frederick Turner's brilliant spiritual history of humankind's ragged journey from simplicity to suppression, the author devotes much discussion to the "Wild Man" who lies at the heart of so much of European mythology –

mythology given substance when Europeans "first burst into this silent, splendid Nature," as British ambassador James Bryce put it at the turn of the century, and discovered the continent occupied by peoples they chose to call primitive — wild. What Turner tells us is that the violence of the response to that encounter was not merely Europeans venting their urge to conquest, but a reaction to the shock of recognition: in the Indians, the first people of the American continent, European culture was presented with all that had been lost when the first dibble stick was jammed into the earth somewhere in the Fertile Crescent to begin agriculture and the first steps in the implacable trek to what conventional wisdom insists is civilization.

Before that moment, human beings had once known something important about themselves and the world around them: that all life was one in the great web of Creation. As the structure of the human community became more centralized and intricately organized in the Mediterranean and then the European worlds, the spiritual character of its relationship to the land slowly evolved through a spiral of increasingly humanistic religious systems until the anthropocentrism of orthodox Judaism and Christianity all but obliterated the traces of its earthly connections. By the time internal forces of empire and restlessness sent Europeans across the ocean to exercise dominion over the lands and people of the "New World," reason had triumphed over myth.

In spite of their own well-developed strains of civilization and complexities of language and culture, most of the first people still possessed that original knowledge and had devised powerful rituals and stories to honor it. The Europeans — and later those who called themselves Americans — might have listened with profit to what the Indians had to tell them about that relationship. In the native residents of the American continent, the European community suddenly was confronted by the common mythic past it had rejected, the wilder half of the shared human experience that presented the Europeans with choices they had almost forgotten how to make. The tragedy, of course, is that when given the opportunity — a second chance — the choices they made were almost invariably those which continued the long alienation from the wilderness that had nurtured their beginnings. It had taken Europeans nearly ten thousand years to separate themselves almost completely from the Wild Man of their origins; encountering him again on this continent, it took them only half a millenium to nearly repeat the process with savagery and oppression.

I say "nearly" because, try as we might, we who are the inheritors of that European experience have never fully been able to escape the memory of the

Wild Man and his message within us. I don't think we want to escape him. An argument could be made that the entire conservation movement in this country has been one long yearning to reclaim that original knowledge – and so has the literary tradition that has evolved with it over more than a century, from Henry David Thoreau telling us that "In Wildness is the preservation of the World" to Edward Abbey reminding us that uncontrolled growth "is the etiology of the cancer cell." In the wildness of the West is the preservation of that yearning. Aldo Leopold told us that we must nurture a land ethic, and in *The Diversity of Life*, E. O. Wilson speaks of what he calls "biophilia," which he defines as the connectedness that human beings subconsciously seek with the rest of life. "To biophilia," he writes, "can be added the idea of wilderness, all the land and communities of plants and animals still unsullied by human occupation. . . . We do not understand ourselves yet and descend further from heaven's air if we forget how much the natural world means to us. Signals abound that the loss of life's diversity endangers not just the body but the spirit."

So it is not just in scenery or history's more colorful trappings that we nonfictionists should find the essence of the West, it is in the quest for connectedness. I have called it a yearning. It could also be called love, still not an easy word to use right out loud, even in the Post-Esalen Age. But I think we who write about the West need to use that word and to accept the fact that the love we feel, each for himself and herself, and for all our brothers and sisters in the human world, inescapably includes the extended circle of the land and the life it holds. Love is, after all, the essence of our joy in witnessing and writing about the life around us – and of the anger, pain, and guilt we feel when we have turned our backs on it. Every time we kill a living thing without honoring what it has given us in its life and now in its death; every time we destroy habitat as we tear things down, build things up, and move things around; every time we push another species into the Black Hole of extinction with our careless enthusiasms – every time we do these things, it is a violation, then, not merely of ethics, but of love, and when writers like me rise up on our hind legs and start bellowing forth outrage, it is because it is not only the land that has been assaulted, but the deepest and most personal part of our own history. The shock of recognition that reverberated in the psyches of the first European invaders is echoed in our own: We have met the Wild Man, and he is us. We have killed the Wild Man – and he is us.

So, even as I continue to honor the history of the West, I now spend most of my time asking us to turn our backs on much of it – to reject that portion of it that would have us continue the old dangerous game of killing the future for the sake of present gain. In the canyon country of southern Utah, as everywhere else, we must learn, finally, that wilderness is not, as our history has insisted, a threat to be conquered but in fact a lesson to be embraced. For in wilderness, as in the eyes of the wild creatures that inhabit it, we find something that binds us firmly to the long history of life on earth, something that can teach us how to live in this place, how to accept our limitations, how to celebrate the love we feel when we let ourselves feel it for all other living creatures. And there is another history to be found in the wild, a history we humans can so far only guess at, and this, too, must be honored. It begins beyond human time, somewhere in the realms where stars are born. It intrigues me, this dimension of time. I would like to tell its history with some of the careless facility with which I have rendered so much human history, but I cannot. I can neither know the history nor tell it. But here in canyon country sometimes I think I can feel it and take strength from it. I will remember, always, the moment when I discovered the dancing image of Kokopelli on a stone in a secret place, the sudden urge I felt then to look over my shoulder to see if some small, dark, shy, ancient person was not watching me from behind the willows of the creek-bed. There was no one, of course, no one whom I could see. But I photographed the image, and a print of that photograph resides above my desk where I can see it at all times. Whatever the precise message its maker wanted to pass along, I know that the antic figure speaks also of time, stone time. I look at it and know that I will return to this place again and again, a place as as central to my knowledge now as all the memories of my life and my family's life, all the history I have learned, all the books I may have read or all the words I may have written.

When I do, I will touch the stone . . . and dream of stars.